Soak it!

...in the Word!

Farikanayi

Dedication

I would like to dedicate this book to everyone who has persisted in doing good in the face of challenges, difficulties, issues, trouble and tough times. The fact that you are holding on means that at the back of your mind you know things will get better. May God reward your tenacity and make you see the end of your faith. Don't give up, don't get discouraged. There really is hope to the living. Whatever you are facing and dealing with will pass. May God give you the confidence to know that this is so, the assurance that His Word which He has sent will heal you, the strength to stand and believe while things may still look dark and the peace which passes all understanding and causes you to smile in the face of adversity. You will make it.

Contents

Acknowledgements

My children inspire me to reach my goals. They inspire me to dream and to want a better life than what I have had to date. For them I want to wring out every bit of creativity, skill and talent that God invested in me and use it all up! I want them to be challenged to fulfil their own destinies at an early age then enjoy the benefits and the rewards of it. My children are a very special blessing that God gave to an undeserving woman; at least that is how I looked at myself. They are the evidence of God's goodness to me. So I acknowledge their role always as the catalysts for my creativity.

Each time I sit down to write I feel like I am more equipped than ever before. God has put people in my life; his anointed servants who tirelessly teach the Word. As I write I know that the understanding and the revelation I now have is not my own. So I appreciate my pastors and all the anointed men and women of God who bring spiritual food to the table so that I can continue to grow in my areas of gifting.

There are always Godly cheerleaders who jump about and shout celebrating us and encouraging us to be the best we can be. I have friends who egg me on, not into mischief (Mmmmm! Lady J what say ye???) but into excellence and I

5

acknowledge their part in making me write. I love them and I thank God for their part in reminding me to write, challenging me to stay on track when I get too busy with other things and reminding me of what I need to do.

My two daddies have each in their own way made me know I am very precious. My earthly father KGD and my heavenly Father have both in unique ways made me know that I am loved. I am grateful that unlike many people I was raised by a good man. I was loved by a good man. I was taught to love the written word by a good man. I acknowledge the unconditional love and the blessing my Father God has showered my life with and that regardless of what has happened in the past, he hasn't listened to people's condemning opinions of me but has loved me with an everlasting love.

Finally I acknowledge the importance and significance of every person who will ever purchase a Farikanayi authored book. May God bless you for the seed you sow in me. As you purchase a book, see it as a seed and expect a harvest. It is your encouragement to a woman who has finally realised just how much she loves to write. Thank you.

Introduction
SOAK IT!

It's amazing how the simple things we do on a daily basis can be sources of lessons that can help us scale the issues and mountains we are dealing with in life. God created the heavens and the earth and he can use anything in his creation as a tool for our help. Unfortunately we are not always expecting or listening. We have become experts at defining how God should speak, when and through which people. We have sometimes lost our ability to be amazed, to be in awe and to be appreciative. As a result God performs his wonders but we don't see or hear unless they fit in with our pre-defined 'voice of The Lord'.

I was cleaning a pan I had roasted some meat in and the gunge was washing off easily after I had soaked it for some time. I started thinking about the impact of soaking and how a few hours of sudsy water had loosened and softened the crusty stuff that had previously lined the pan. An image of our dirt- encrusted lives being soaked in God's goodness then came to my mind. How easily all the gunk and grease that attaches itself to people can be removed if God is allowed into the equation so that it is he that does the soaking and loosening of all the goo.

Being human, we scrub, scour, scrape and rub hoping that these human methods can be translated to everything in life from dirty dishes to dirty or burdened lives. We don't always realise that our rubbing and scrubbing doesn't work with spiritual things. We can't always paddle our way out of the situations we find ourselves in. Think about how frantically the disciples paddled and scooped when their boat was hit by a storm. They tried to offer a natural solution to a problem that needed the voice of the master. He didn't paddle, he didn't scream, he didn't panic. All he did was speak to the storm and it obeyed (Mark 4:39). Scrapping and scouring doesn't even really work with pans sometimes so why we think it can work in spiritual matters is a wonder.

But the principle of soaking applies to natural and spiritual things. The question is simply what you are soaking the thing in and for how long. Soapy water loosens tough dirt. Detergents and bleach also help deal with things that won't wash off with water. The soaking itself is great but its impact and effectiveness is then multiplied and magnified based on what you put into partnership with it and how long you leave it well alone so that it can get to work. Soaking combined with an agent and time does wonders in the natural and it does the same in spiritual matters as well.

Looking through the bible one comes across a kaleidoscope of lived experiences and various ways people address or rather attempt to address the issues that are dragging them down, the cumbersome baggage they lug around, the inflicted pain and hurt they haven't managed to shift and the issues that have emanated from both their own mistakes and the mistakes of those around them.

There are endless stories of people who tried to sort things out their own way and failed dismally. They made bad situations worse and they started domino-effected catastrophes that impact current generations centuries after their inception. Their pride, foolishness, disobedience and bad choices did not solve the problems and we can study these lives not gleefully or self-righteously but humbly acknowledging that there but for the grace of God.... We can only be grateful that it is not our own lives that have been immortalised in print for global and trans-generational perusal. We wouldn't fare any better than Samson, Peter, Thomas, Rahab, Sarah, Hagar, Abram and the host and cloud of witnesses presented to us in God's word (Hebrews 12:1). Rather than vilify them we can appreciate the lessons they provide, the warnings they flash at us.

Alongside the apparent 'failures', there are those to whom we readily attribute the tag of success. We have the Ruths and Esthers, the Joshuas and Calebs, the Hannahs and Elizabeths, the guileless Nathaniels and that concoction of perfection we see as we find Deborah and Jael, John the Baptist and other examples of biblical success stories. From these we don't get condemnation or even a yardstick too long for us. Instead as their victories are elaborated upon so is their humanity revealed, not to disparage them but rather to give us anchorage into their lives, to allow us to see that our frailty does not disqualify us, and also to help us remain grounded, knowing that even in the most gifted and skilled of us lurks the human element which doubts and sometimes fails to see things the way God does.

As we explore various lives and their paddling and scraping, we also hopefully identify the most effective soaking agents we can use to help us handle the challenges we deal with on a daily basis. Just like we don't always just use soapy water but sometimes have to find tougher cleaning products to sort out tough dirt, we find out that even in our lives, there are different things we can use also to soak the tough issues we contend with.

1

SOAK IT!

Before exploring the wonderful soakers, the people who found Godly ways to address their issues, let's briefly consider those who didn't fare so well. They will be accorded only one chapter because the focus should not really be on them but on solutions, on finding out how to soak and with what to soak our lives, pain, hurts, mistakes, challenges, problems and grease.

Some people have been dealing with issues that were started by their parents or grandparents. Maybe you are dealing with financial ruin which started because an ancestor drank and gambled away the family wealth. Or maybe a stubborn parent refused to seek financial advice and mis-invested and lost everything the family owned. The children may now be trying to pick up the pieces but they have no natural examples of handling finances in a Godly way. Some children may have been dealing with illnesses passed down by parents because of undisciplined lifestyles. Many people are dealing with issues with generational origins, they have been long-standing and now it is difficult to just scrape their lives clean.

By God's grace and with his love and unmerited support and sustenance I have raised four children. Looking back over their lives I can recall things they did which they then tried to correct the best way they knew how. What may have started off as a little thing in some cases ended up being a catastrophe because they didn't realise that they didn't need to solve or sort out things on their own. They scrubbed and scoured and tried to deal with whatever challenges they had but the harder they paddled usually the worse the issues became. My kids are not an exception in this, talk to thousands, in fact millions of parents who daily perform mop-up operations after their children have been arrested, started using drugs, have hooked up with bad people, have become drunks or the local loose girls, have become pregnant or made someone pregnant, have got into serious debt and a myriad other situations that cause pain, conflict and anger in families.

Sometimes grandma really does know best, she has lived longer; she has made the mistakes young people think are unique to them and their generation. The fact that grandma has lived past her 60th birthday may just be testament to the fact that she discovered methods of degreasing issues that actually work. Grandma in this case could represent parents, good church leaders, good friends and above all the Word of God. But people prefer to scrub and scrape, they want to paddle and scour never realising that there may be better, easier and more effective ways to deal with life's traumas and that those who have lived to tell it just might be worth listening to.

So you may be looking at the pan that is your life and there is a lot of greasy gunge stuck to it. It's disgusting stuff that you can't live with because it smells and it is unsightly. It has also stuck so hard you don't know what to do to get rid of it. You may have been pretending that all is well, putting on your best smile for everyone. But accumulated issues have a way of becoming visible and a time comes when the smile becomes very thin. Well you are not the only one, many have been where you are, analysing and assessing their lives for solutions. Not all their responses have been useful or helpful, they have either made the issues even more complex or they have ended up with bigger messes than when they began. It could be they have scraped so hard that they have damaged the pan they are supposed to clean. What you are facing may appear new to you but there is nothing new under the sun (Ecclesiastes 1:9) and what is tempting you now is actually considered common to all men (1 Corinthians 10:13). So others have been through it and lived, so can you. Just stop scrapping, scrubbing and paddling. Soak.

Mark 4:35-41 is a good example of good people seeking human solutions to their predicament. Their boat was taking in water and they were scared. There was a storm, a situation they couldn't control and they felt that they were in trouble. So they started dealing with the problem, they started bailing and paddling but the boat still sank. Their common sense methods did not keep them afloat; in fact it was a whole lot of worry for nothing because their situation did not improve. Like most of us when things get difficult we forget the very word that will take us through the valley of the shadow of death (Psalm 23) and we start listening to words from people who are in similar situations to us. We start comparing notes as if that will make the problem go away. If they knew any better wouldn't they be out of the mess as well? How can you get financial advice from a broke person, one who is in even more debt than you? They have yet to prove their financial intelligence. Be intelligent enough to see that they can't help you, they also need help. The little teenage friend you are confiding in and covering for each other with is as ignorant about life as you are. They have only lived for as long as you have. What makes you think they are any wiser than you are? Why do you give credence to their 'wisdom' over that of your parents?

Another useful illustration is the incident involving a young king called Rehoboam who ignored the counsel of old men who had been with his father Solomon choosing instead to be advised by young men who had grown up with him, his peers (1 Kings 12). As a result, his people rebelled against him. He lost a sizable chunk of a kingdom that should have been his. Similarly the disciples listened to the voice of the storm, the howling of the wind and forgot the words of their master who had already told them in Mark 4:35 that they were passing over not into the sea but to the other side. The storm muffled the voice whose power and healing they had already witnessed in many ways.

Maybe you can think back or even not so far back into issues that have robbed you of your sleep and your peace. Yet you woke up in the morning and your worry and stress hadn't changed the issue one aorta, if anything things were even tougher because you were now trying to address them from blood-shot eyes and a befuddled, sleep-deprived brain. Your worry accomplished squat!

Jesus was on the boat with the disciples but he did not help with the paddling. In fact he was asleep. When the disciples woke him up he asked what all the flurry of activity and fear was about. He then faced the storm and told it to behave, he ordered it to be still and it obeyed (Mark 4:39). A supernatural, Godly solution was needed and it was a word from The Lord, the Man from Galilee, the Man who stilled and still stills the water, the fourth man who appeared in the fiery furnace (Daniel 3:25). He didn't need to manoeuvre and manipulate the situation; in fact he didn't need to engage with it at all by talking about it and fretting over it. Instead he spoke to it and told it what to do:

He got up, rebuked the wind and said to the waves, "Quiet! Be still!" Then the wind died down and it was completely calm (Mark 4:39).

King David is a good example of a paddler. He messed up big time when he acted on his lust for Bathsheba. Then the paddling really began. He orchestrated a disastrous bail-out scheme which led to pain, shame, death and untold grief and suffering. He tried to launch a kingly clean-up operation which did not leave a clean pan but rather led to rotting stench all around him, his palace and the family he hurt. God's friend used lies, deceit, manipulation and every scheming tactic he could to hide his sin, but 2 Samuel 11 shows us that the grease did not budge. A lie cannot rescue another lie. The father of lies (John 8:44) does not operate that way. He steals kills and destroys (John 10:10). And so David and Bathsheba along with innocent Uriah all paid a horrendous price for trying to scour and scrub the pan of their lust.

Think about all the political scandals that have gone totally out of hand as politicians and other people in positions of influence have lied, killed, threatened and bribed as ways to paddle their way out of trouble. But the harder they scraped the more stubborn the issues became and the stench couldn't be hidden for long regardless of how much PR perfumes were sprayed. In the end, all their effort and all their fame and money could not camouflage their mess. Unfortunately because of their positions in society, their fall was of Humpty Dumpty proportions scattering bits and pieces everywhere and usually affecting the lives of many people in the process.

Before we all sit in our self-righteous seats of judgment we can also look at our own lives and how all our efforts to deal with our issues in our own little human ways have almost always led to serious disaster. The times we have thought we knew more than the Creator of the heavens and the earth, the times we have not involved him in our decisions, the times we have not 'inquired of The Lord' (1 Samuel 30:8) we have ended up lost and disillusioned and sometimes blaming God for not rescuing us from messes we created. He gets blamed for our mistakes; he gets blamed when we have excluded him from our dealings. When things are going well for us, we are in the seats of honor and he does not exist.

Let's explore some serial paddlers, our parents in the faith Sarah and Abraham. How many times did they try to deal with their issues through lies, manipulation, anger, doubt and disbelief? How many times did other people suffer because of something they did? In case you are not familiar with this awesome but very human couple, a few examples will be highlighted for your benefit:

In Genesis 12 Abram told the Egyptians that Sarai was his sister. The Pharaoh took her but his whole household was struck down with disease until he returned Sarai to her husband.

In Genesis 20 Abraham lied and said that Sarah was his sister. Sarah went along with it. God spoke to Abimelech and warned him that his death was imminent if he didn't return Abraham's wife to him. At this point every woman in Abimelech's household had also been struck down with barrenness because of Abraham's paddling to save his own life.

In Genesis 26 Abraham's son Isaac shows he has inherited his father's paddling ability so he also lies and calls his wife his sister.

When the miracle seemed to tarry, Sarah started paddling. In Genesis 16 she gave her slave Hagar to Abram to be his wife so that she could have a child through her.   Her meddling, scrubbing and manipulation and Abram's acquiescence led to pain, jealousy, strife, discord and the birth of a nation of people referred to by the Angel of The Lord in these words in Genesis 16:12:

He will be a wild donkey of a man; his hand will be against everyone and   everyone's hand against him, and he will live in hostility toward all his brothers

There is more that could be said about Abram laughing when he was told that he would have a child through his wife Sarai (Genesis 17:17) Sarah also laughed and lied when confronted about her lack of faith (Genesis 18:12). We know that in many places in the new Testament Sarah and Abraham are held up for us as role models in faith. That is what God's grace does. When he covers our lives and soaks them in his grace, all that is left is the perfection he created. He washes us clean of all unrighteousness (1 John 1:9).

We really need to allow the great cloud of witnesses to speak to us (Hebrews 12:1). Their voices can save us so much pain and heartache. Their lived experiences can be our learning material, a compass that shows us where to go but also where not to go, what to do and what not to do.

How easy it is for us to look at people like Jacob and Gideon and many others who appeared to be quite lacking in faith sometimes and judge them. It's easy to analyse someone else's failings without seeing our own.

The woman at the well is a relevant example to explore (John 4). She met the one man who could quench her thirst and stop her continuing on her bed-hopping marathon. She soaked her issues in wrong relationships and the fact that she kept moving from one to the next demonstrated the ineffectiveness of the relationships in removing or addressing whatever was bugging her. She soaked her life in what she may have thought of as love but which turned out to be something else. Only when she met The Lord of lords, the Prince of peace did she stop in her tracks and receive the true thirst-quenching solutions to her circumstances.

Maybe you have only been married twice or three times, maybe you have remained single but you have been in and out of relationships like a child playing hopscotch. Either way, you are paddling and you know it because the end of each relationship makes you feel as if you have lost a part of yourself, and maybe you have. But bed-hopping does not solve the issues you face, it does not scratch the itch you have. Turn around and look to the author and perfecter of your faith (Hebrews 12:2), let him offer the supernatural solutions you need.

Think back to Ananias and Sapphira in Acts 5. Instead of taking time to find out what genuine giving was, they decided to do some scouring and some scrapping so that they could appear as if they were serving God wholeheartedly through their giving. They cooked the books as one might say so that the percentage they gave would appear to be 100%. They assumed that they could trick the omnipotent, omniscient and omnipresent God into accepting what appeared to be their best and they paid with their lives. They didn't have to give 100%. They could have given 50% and stated that it was 50%

and that would have been perfect. But they wanted to give the impression that they were 100% givers. How many times do people get into debt just so that they can give their neighbours the impression that they are in a particular income bracket when they are not? Ananias and Sapphira were busy paddling because they thought that God needed to be impressed the same way a man, or woman might lie to give the impression that he is who or what he is not. They paid with their lives, their scheming, rubbing and scratching was all to naught and for naught. God was not impressed.

One of the prayers I make on a regular basis, maybe not so much now because God has helped me deal with the issue, is a prayer for right motives. I am a very active person in many ways. I don't like being idle. I am also the sort of person who commits to things and people. If something needs to be done I will do it. But a few years ago I realised that I didn't always do things, particularly so in God's house for the right reasons. I realised that the bible expects me to do everything I do not as unto people but as unto The Lord. So for quite a while I would always check with The Lord, I would pray and ask him to help me do things, serve, give, participate for the right reasons. I wanted him to light up my heart so that when I served there were no ulterior motives lurking around, no wanting to be seen, no wanting to be applauded, no wanting to appear better than anybody else. It took a while but I realised that the more I opened my heart to his searchlight the less I needed to impress. I want to always serve because I love God. Whether people see or comment is immaterial. The all-seeing God sees and that is what matters. Ananias and Sapphira wanted human accolade. So they lied and they died.

Human methods and antics rarely ever solve the issues we deal with in life. Wisdom is about knowing where to put your trust and your hope. A fool says in his heart that there is no God (Psalm 14:1). I suppose there is also an element of foolishness in not asking for God's help when it is freely available to us.

God is our refuge and strength, an ever-present help in trouble (Psalm 46:1).

Our capabilities are finite, There is a point we should reach where we acknowledge and admit that we don't have the capacity mentally, physically, spiritually or financially to solve our problems. We then have to surrender each issue to someone who is bigger than us and who can give us the help we need. The more we paddle and scour the more usually we make a mess of things. Soaking involves letting go, not interfering and leaving things well alone. It means getting along with other things knowing that the one you have entrusted with your children, problems, finances, life, career, marriage is well able to sort it out and return it to you value added, better than when you left it at his feet. It also involves giving the Word, prayer, patience and persistence time to loosen the gunge we are dealing with.

It's important that we loosen our fingers from the issues we are gripping close to our chests. We have to release our lives to God and let him work in us without our help or interference. Stop yo-yoing with the problem, to God, back to you, to God, back to you. Leave it with the potter. He knows what to do to make it whole again.

2

SOAK IT!

A perfunctory prayer is okay because I suppose it is better than no prayer. But it is the effective fervent prayer of the righteous that avails much (James 5:16 NKJV). I believe that some prayers are a waste of time because if we pray amiss we get no results, so those kinds of prayers it would appear according to James 4:3 are a waste of time.

It's funny how everyone prays regardless of their belief system. Every person at some point in their life utters some form of prayer. Some pray to Jehovah, the Almighty, the Creator and origin of all things. Others have deviated from the Creator to the created. They have been bewitched by 'attractive' and more politically correct forms of worship that entice and ensnare and they have been hoodwinked by false teachers and have started worshipping other gods. Psalm 115 describes these gods:

2. Why do the nations say, "Where is their God?"

25

3. Our God is in heaven; he does whatever pleases him.
4. But their idols are silver and gold, made by human hands.
5. They have mouths, but cannot speak, eyes, but cannot see.
6. They have ears, but cannot hear, noses, but cannot smell.
7. They have hands, but cannot feel, feet, but cannot walk,
    nor can they utter a sound with their throats.
8. Those who make them will be like them, and so will all who
    trust in them.

When it's described so clearly and succinctly, it makes me realise how daft we can be as human beings. We make something then we ascribe to it powers of the divine. We shape some of the idols after created things, made by God less dramatically than our own creation and we start worshipping those things. These are the very things created for our benefit, to provide us with food and shelter, to beautify our environment, to be under our dominion (Genesis 1:26) but instead grown men and women bow to these very things in servitude, it is mind-boggling.

I don't think people always realise that the things they work hard to possess end up possessing them and becoming their gods. These gods don't have to be statues and idols made to look like animals. Anything that thwarts true worship and directs glory from God to itself can be a god. A television can be a god if it takes pre-eminence over everything else, if people can't go to church because there is a show they *have* to watch, if family time takes the backbench to the remote control. Jobs, money, relationships, alcohol, drugs and food can all be gods as can positions and peers.

A relationship that takes over your life to the point where your family becomes enemies, your friends become alienated and it becomes just you and that person can be a god, a very possessive god who takes over your loyalty and directs it only to itself. A good relationship always seeks what is best for you, it doesn't try to isolate you, it is not in competition with your loved ones and it does not seek to change you but rather to reinforce who you are, who God made you. So check out what has started stealing your time, your character, your values and your judgment. Keep in mind that the devil comes to kill to steal and to destroy (John 10:10). If relationships with your family start dying as soon as you get into a relationship with someone, you may need to check out whose agent they are. If you can't openly be the Christian you are and you have to tone down your faith and your confession, you may have got yourself hooked to the enemy.

Hannah in (1 Samuel 1) was unhappy about the state of affairs in her life. She wanted to be a mother but she simply could not conceive. Her husband loved her but his love could not quench her desire to be a mother. She refused to be pacified, refused to accept a situation she knew to be less than what she wanted. She didn't believe in those who said 'At least....'. She knew who she was and what God's promises were for her and she refused to accept anything less. So she soaked her situation in prayer.

Added to her barrenness, her inability to produce, Hannah had another taunting enemy in the form of her husband's other wife Peninah (1 Samuel 1:6). Hannah could have responded in kind, turning their household into a place of bickering and squabbling. But instead she turned to the One who has the power to open wombs (Genesis 30:22; Psalm113:9). She soaked her issues in prayer and God heard and responded not by giving her just the one child but five more (1 Samuel 2:21).

It's funny how looking at my life and that of the people God has crossed my path with that sometimes we respond to life's issues foolishly. We don't always learn from this virtuous woman called Hannah. We are too busy telling everybody about our business that we don't get the chance to speak to the One who can make a difference for us. We are so busy whinging and grumbling we don't realise that the same time we are whinging could be time spent in prayer. So we perpetuate problems whose impact could be curtailed if we took them to the right person, to God.

I think back to my mother's life. She went home just over a year ago and one of the things that remains fixed in my mind is how much she relied on God. She prayed daily for her family. She fasted at least once a week and covered us all in prayer. Regardless of what anybody might say or think, I believe that members of our immediate and extended family have lived blessed lives in part because of the prayer cover of this awesome prayer warrior. She was never a very talkative person; she didn't talk to many people about her life. She didn't seek many friendships. She guarded the things that were precious to her sharing them with her God because she knew that he could make a difference.

Interesting comparisons can be drawn between Hannah, Sarai and Rachel. All three were barren and all three wanted to have children. They responded differently to their situation:

> Sarai introduced her maid to her marriage bed. She let another woman sleep with her husband so that she could have a child through her. She coined the issue of surrogacy. In her desperation she ignored or undermined the impact of her actions, she became temporarily blind to the devastating effects of her choices (Genesis 16).

Rachel wanted a child; in fact she was desperate for a child. But she didn't seem to know where to go to have her barrenness dealt with. So she became a nag. She pestered her husband as if he had a child hidden away in a safe, but he knew that he wasn't a womb-opener so he referred her to the One who was her help, the One who could solve her problem (Genesis 30).

Hannah also wanted to have a child and she went into the temple of The Lord to pray until she got her answer (1 Samuel 1).

It's so easy for us to condemn Sarah and Rachel, to look down our noses as if we could never stoop so low as to do what they did. But we have brought our own share of Hagars into the areas where we have been barren. We have maneuvered, borrowed, withheld, manipulated and in our own ways failed to trust and appeal to the One who has the power to help us. But Hannah prayed until she got her expected and desired result, she held on to the promises of God. She got what she prayed for. She became a mother many times over.

Like Hannah we can also talk to our heavenly father and ask of him whatsoever we need (1 John 5:15) knowing that he hears us and grants our petitions.

Luke 2:37 talks about Anna the widow who 'never left the temple but worshiped night and day, fasting and praying'. Anna was a widow, widowed after just seven years in marriage. She must have been a young woman, capable of remarrying and moving on with her life the way most people would. But she chose a different path for her life. Instead of becoming a statistic, someone who needed looking after, she chose instead a more excellent way (1 Corinthians 12:31) and decided to spend her days, years, decades, her very life in the house of The Lord soaking not only her own life but that of people around her in prayer.

Imagine being a permanent fixture in the temple, like the stained glass windows we see in most old churches. People knew that if they went into the house of The Lord they would see Anna. She was consistent and constant in her ministry and in her prayers. She soaked her life in prayer and in the end her expectation was not cut off (Proverbs 23:18), she got to see The Lord.

When bad things happen people don't always turn to The Lord. In fact a lot of the time they rebel, they blame God and they decide to act as if their pain is very unique. I know because even now as a 'mature' believer I still try to sort things out my own way when I am in a tight spot. If a believer who is in a position of authority does something wrong God is blamed. People don't seem to want to blame people, they use any excuse they can to blame God for things that are done by people who have a brain and make decisions which are sometimes quite silly. So next time something goes wrong, let's immediately turn to The Lord and ask for his help. Before picking up that phone to call friends and relatives, let's call The Lord.

But here is Anna, a young widow who could have followed in the footsteps of many who were angry and bitter dragging through life in full blame mode. But she changed location. She moved from her home to her father's house. She decided to soak her life in prayer instead of wallowing in self-pity, bitterness, denial and whatever emotions we promote when things aren't going our way. I know what it feels like when a marriage ends due to divorce or death. Some people have to deal with loss of jobs, status, income, opportunities or relationships. Whatever it is that has caused a change of status is not bigger than God. Widowhood, divorce, being an orphan, being let down, being cheated or cheated on, none of these are bigger than God so we can boldly approach the throne of grace knowing that he is capable of helping us and delivering us from whatever issues we are dealing with (Hebrews 4:16).

I'm curious about why God needed this widow Anna to be placed in Luke 2. There must have been other widows during her time but she is mentioned by name. She soaked her life in prayer. She made a decision not to stagnate, decay or waste away in sadness and depression at losing her husband at such an early age. She did the unexpected choosing to remove herself also from the sympathetic, patronizing voices and stares. People's well-meaning comments can ensnare us. As they express their sadness at our loss or pain, they don't always bring solutions but focus on highlighting what is wrong. Moving away from the marital home meant that if anyone wanted to see Anna they had to go to the house of her God, they had to go to the temple. She moved form he place of loss to her place of strength.

It would be interesting to look at our lives and see how we have responded during our times of trials and challenges. I know my reaction has not always been honourable. I have responded with anger, bitterness, offense, jealousy, shame and sometimes I have just not responded at all allowing despondency to set in as I felt hopeless and helpless in the face of issues I thought were too big for me. Some people turn to drinking and drugs, others turn to unsuitable relationships, some rebel in anger and make decisions that only worsen the challenge they are dealing with. Anna responded by relocating to a place where she could serve God and pray without disturbance.

I wonder how we could change the trajectory of our lives if instead of trying to manipulate our situations we simply relocated. This might be physical relocation or a change in attitude. One way or the other we do need to relocate, we may need to flee from some of our associates because of the places they take us. We may have to make a conscious effort to end some friendships because they want to live in the past and want to drag us along that path.

For whatever reason prophetess Anna chose to soak her whole life in prayer and worship and she was kept around long enough to see the end of her faith (1 Peter 1:9). Her hope was not deferred (Proverbs 13:12).

Jabez is another biblical witness of someone who soaked his life in prayer. He was in a tight spot:
Jabez cried out to the God of Israel, "Oh, that you would bless me and enlarge my territory! Let your hand be with me, and keep me from harm so that I will be free from pain." And God granted his request.

Jabez' mother had given him a name based on the circumstances of his birth.

She took instructions from her circumstances, from what she was going through. As if that was not enough she prophesied trouble over her son, instead of calling him 'Blessed' as a prophetic utterance for him, she decided to succumb to the pain of her circumstances and there are many parents who have wronged their children by naming them based on their challenges and pain. Jabez' mother didn't have the revelation that our words have power, that they are prophetic, they cause things to happen. Instead of naming her son well, in a prophetic way that would bring him out of the pain she bore him in, she prophesied instead to more pain.

Thank God Jabez knew that God was the only one that could reverse this negative prophecy. Like Anna he soaked his life in prayer asking for God to change the situation he was in and deliver him from what appeared to be his reality and destiny. Because he didn't just cry and complain, but prayed, God heard his prayer and granted his request. Jabez prayed a prayer that yielded results.

We have that same avenue of help also available to us. Whatever is happening in our lives, we can soak it all in prayer like Hannah, Anna and Jabez. We know that God is the same yesterday, today and forever (Hebrews 13:8), so if he heard the prayers of our brothers and sisters in biblical times, he will also hear and grant our requests. He is unchanging (Hebrews 6:17).

3

Sirophonecian woman soaked it in persistence

S O A K   I T!

Most people give up when they face tough situations. They blame God and go off in a huff because they assume that he has left them even though he succinctly tells us that he will never leave us nor forsake us (Hebrews 13:5; Joshua 1:5; Deuteronomy 31:6). They think that God is only with them when things are going right, when they are celebrating, when they are victorious. They read aspects of the Word omitting such scriptures as these:

I was young and now I am old, yet I have never seen the righteous forsaken or their children begging bread (Psalm 37:25)

The righteous person may have many troubles, but The Lord delivers him from them all (Psalm 34:19)

God is our refuge and strength, an ever-present help in trouble (Psalm 46:1)

These are just a few of the scriptures that are double sided; they assure us that there are times when trouble will haunt us, but then they don't leave us wallowing in despair, they also assure us that God brings us the answers and the deliverance we need to emerge from those issues and circumstances. Trouble will come, but so will our helper. There is no need to give up but there is every need to persist in believing, in praying, asking, receiving and trusting like Sarah and Abraham that he is faithful who promised (1 Thessalonians 5:24; Hebrews 10:23).

God knows that when things are tough we will need help. Some issues are too big for us, too painful, to complex, too hard. So he tells us in Psalm 46 that he is a **very present help** in times of trouble. He is not a long distance help, he is not a perfunctory or lip-service help. He is a very present help for us when we are in trouble. We need to go to him when we are in trouble, not to people, not to ourselves but to our very present helper.

One of the most precious scriptures in the bible is the well-known Psalm 23.

Many of us memorized it in Sunday school and many have sung about it. But instead of referring to it when we are in need of encouragement, we have made it a common set of words which appear to be devoid of power. That is a shame because Psalm 23 is packed with promises we can claim for just about every situation we face in our lives. We can draw from it knowing that first of all God is our shepherd. That is enough to stop right there and rest in his love. As my shepherd he takes care of where I go, when I go there, when I eat, what I eat, who is allowed access to me, my daily timetable. He is responsible for every aspect of my being! Without even reading further, the knowledge that he is our shepherd should be enough to help our blood pressure come down to normal levels, enough for our hearts to settle in peace, enough for our minds to stop imagining horror story events. We have a shepherd who loves us and is capable of looking after us, guiding us, blessing us, providing for us, anointing us. So next time the issues of life try to overwhelm our peace, we can turn them all over to our shepherd and lie down in peaceful green pastures with a restored soul.

I am always amazed that there are people who never pray, never go to church, never do anything to show that they believe in God, yet when they face difficulties the port of blame is the God they neglect. It's almost as if they keep him in a locked cupboard and only bring him out when they need a punching bag. Yet they expect him to be there cleaning up after them, rescuing them from their mess even though they do not want a relationship with him. They are God-abusers using him as their punch-bag when they are frustrated or when their cleverness turns out to be nothing more than foolishness. When their plans fail they are not to blame, God is.

The Sirophonecian woman was made of sterner faith stuff than that! She did not give up on God. In fact when it appeared Christ was not going to respond to her issue she went into a serious presentation of her case. She soaked her situation in wisdom, courage (speaking up and challenging what The Lord Jesus said!), determination and focus. In the end The Lord himself admitted that she was a woman of great faith. He granted her request and her child was healed (Matthew 15:25-28).

What would have happened if this woman became offended at The Lord's words, at his implication that giving her this gift of healing was like casting bread to the dogs (Matthew 15:26; Mark 7:27)? What if she analysed his words and was so affronted she stormed off! Her child would probably have died or continued to suffer, she would have probably become a bitter woman, the her conversation with The Lord would not have been recorded for it to become an encouragement to us so many years after it happened. But she kept pressing like Paul mentioned in Philippians 3:14:

I press on toward the goal to win the prize for which God has called me heavenward in Christ Jesus.

Like Paul she identified a goal, a target and she decided that her child was going to be healed. She was prepared to be persistent; she was going to get what she came to The Lord for. And so she soaked her issue is persistence, in conversation with someone who seemed to be insulting her but who also had the answer to her problem. She wasn't so thin-skinned and arrogant like Naaman who thought being told to go and dip himself in the Jordan was beneath him even if the end result would be that he would be leprosy-free (2 Kings 5).

How many financial, spiritual, physical, relational, business issues, how many children have we left to horrible fates or even to death because we became offended and walked off? How many marriages have we allowed to die? How many businesses have we aborted? How many friendships that could have been support networks have we walked away from in a huff because some truth was told us in love but we were not ready to receive it? Are we staying in prayer until we get what we are asking our father or are we storming off in despair because he didn't look at us and give us what we wanted straight away?

This Sirophonecean woman's persistence is worth emulating. We should soak every situation in persistence. We cannot afford to give up on our children's salvation, on our families, on our dreams, on our gifts and talents, on our businesses, on our lives. Regardless of how tough things become we cannot choose death over life. God will not leave us nor will he forsake us (Hebrews 13:5; Joshua 1:5; Deuteronomy 31:6). But we have to stay until he tells us that our children are well, our businesses are healthy, and our relationships are mended. If need be then we stand there and present our case, argue our case before him. After all he is the one who tells us to come and reason with him:

Come now, let us reason together, says The Lord: though your sins are like scarlet, they shall be as white as snow; though they are red like crimson, they shall become like wool (Isaiah 1:18 ESV)

Review the past for me, let us argue the matter together; state the case for your innocence (Isaiah 43:26).

These scriptures don't present or represent us as being in the right. In them we see ourselves clearly as faulty and as having situations that need addressing. But we also see a father who does not want distance between us and him. He calls us to him. He invites us to a conversation with him. Before we even start talking he is already spelling out the outcome for us, whether it is in the form of being proved innocent or in the case of being forgiven. Either way he wants communication and as we draw close he reassures us that all is well.

Jacob sets a good example of persistence. When he knew that something was important to him, time had no meaning anymore. He was prepared to soak it all in persistence and go for what he wanted, what he believed to be his.

These illustrations show this tenacity in his life:

- He was prepared to work for more than a decade for the woman he wanted to have as his wife (Genesis 29)
- He wrestled with an angel or with God and would not let him go until he blessed him even though they wrestled all night (Genesis 32:24-31)

- When his father-in-law tricked him, Jacob did not give up, he found a way to become wealthy even while he was in a place of servitude (Genesis 30)

I suppose in Jacob's case there were other attitudes besides persistence; there was an element of conmanship, some not so trustworthy traits. But he did go for what he wanted even if at times the boundaries between honour and dishonour became quite blurred.

It's very easy for us all to look back at this man Jacob and discuss him in our bible study groups. It is easy to talk about his trickery and quote scriptures at and about him. But if we would remove the logs from our own eyes (Matthew 7:5; Luke 12:56) maybe then we could actually learn from Jacob. Yes we still need to see the rather unsavoury methods he used and acknowledge them as wrong. But we also need to look at his persistence, doggedness and resolution and see if maybe we could learn to persist when things seem to be falling apart. Since we are on the outside looking in we can decide to be persistent without using unfair balances (Proverbs 20:23), we can decide to focus our eyes on the author and perfecter of our faith (Hebrews 12:2) without having to cheat or lie. We can use Jacob's life as an excellent learning tool both to learn what to do and also what not to do.

When Peter was imprisoned (Acts 12:3), the church gathered together. They knew that their persistent prayer was the only way they could help Peter. None of them had the financial or political clout to unlock the prison gates, but they knew the One who sets prisoners free the One who by his word sets all men free, free indeed (John 8:36). So they persisted in their prayers and intercession for their brother Peter and God heard them and released Peter, the same way he will release any of us from financial, physical, health, relational or any other type of situation that is encasing us and preventing us from living the life of liberty he wants us to.

We live in a time when people prefer anything that is instant to doing things through process. So we have instant cake mixes, instant coffees, instant stardom and instant success stories. Everyone clamours for these and so hard work and persistence appear out-moded because we are being hit on all sides with instant everything. Rather than grow vegetables we can walk into a supermarket and find not just a pack of vegetables but we find them washed and 'ready-to-eat'. We even get them already seasoned and sometimes all we have to do is put them in a microwave and blitz them for a few minutes and eat. We are used to things happening quickly so anything that then requires hard work and persistence is wearying. Even relationships are affected. People meet and after a week they are moving in together. They can't even try and develop the relationship and get to know each other. They meet up and sleep up. Within a short time they realise their mistake and start the process again with someone else.

Delilah and Samson's first wife also soaked their issues in persistence. They wore the man of God down till he gave in to their demands. Persistence pays, but they used theirs to destroy and to meet their own selfish demands:

With such nagging she prodded him day after day until he was sick to death of it (Judges 16:16).

Samson had no chance with these naggers, he seemed to have a knack for attracting the sort of women described in various verses in the book of Proverbs:

Better a small serving of vegetables with love than a fattened calf with hatred (Proverbs 15:17)
Better to live on a corner of the roof than share a house with a quarrelsome wife (Proverbs 21:9)

Better to live in a desert than with a quarrelsome and nagging wife (Proverbs 21:19)

Better to live on a corner of the roof than share a house with a quarrelsome wife (Proverbs 25:24)

A quarrelsome wife is like the dripping of a leaky roof in a rainstorm (Proverbs 27:15)

It is so easy to condemn and judge Samson but his life reflects a frequent occurrence. When abused women remarry they seem to go for the same sort of guy as the one they fled from. This can drive their loved ones crazy as they wonder what is wrong with their daughter or sister. They hate being abused yet they fall for abusers and this seems to be the same problem Samson had. He didn't learn from his first marital mistake, he seemed to have pressed a marital repeat button so he went from one manipulative and nagging woman to the next.

We can't keep making the same decisions expecting a different outcome. If you go to a bar to look for a man or woman, you get the bar calibre of person. If you pick some stranger off the street chances are that you have invited some strange stuff into your life. Samson did not go back to God's promises for him to check if maybe his wife-search should change. His first marriage alone should have showed him that he didn't have the wisdom for such an important decision and that maybe he needed to involve his parents and seek their direction, after all they are the people God spoke to about Samson's future (Judges 13).

So maybe before you castigate Samson take time to ask yourself how you are seeking friendships and relationships, how you are networking for your business to grow, where you are going to seek answers for your life. If these are important decisions to you then you need to be serious about the choices you are making the connections you are bringing into your life, the people you are allowing into your inner circle.

Persistence is crucial for anything to last. It is crucial in marriages. It is crucial in parenting and in setting up and running businesses. But it also has to be walking hand in hand with wisdom and with integrity otherwise it translates into abuse, into trickery and into cheating and manipulation.

Proverbs 21:5 uses a different term but the meaning is still linked to persistence, to not giving up, to continuing until the desired results are seen:

The plans of the diligent lead to profit as surely as haste leads to poverty

Haste is the desire for things to happen instantly, now, quickly. Diligence involves taking time to do whatever it takes for desired outcomes to be seen.

Haste does not take time to analyse or prepare a case, it crashes through fences never realising that there are gates that are open if someone just takes time to walk and find them. Haste does not count the cost or realise that the damaged fences will then need to be fixed, the damage repaired.

Persistence may mean getting the results a bit later, but the quality is not compromised. It embraces another virtue, patience and together expected outcomes are reached;

Through patience a ruler can be persuaded, and a gentle tongue can break a bone (Proverbs 25:15)

4

The 70 soaked it in peace

SOAK IT!

In Luke 10 there is an account of Jesus sending the 70 into surrounding areas. He spelt out how they were to conduct themselves when they got there. The core of his instructions though included peace.

They were to speak peace in whatever house they entered. But this was not the end of the instruction. They then had to see if their peace was received. If the 'son of peace' was in that house (verse 6, KJV) then their peace also remained and they were supposed to stay in that house.

There are interesting and important things that leap out from this interchange. One is the fact that Christ expected his disciples to dwell in places where there was peace, where what they brought from him was received and reciprocated. We know this is so from John 14:27 and 2 Thessalonians 3:16:

Peace I leave with you; my peace I give you. I do not give to you as the world gives. Do not let your hearts be trouble and do not be afraid.

Now may The Lord of peace himself give you peace at all times and in every way. The Lord be with you.

So the Prince of Peace wanted the disciples to locate him, to locate people that were like him, households that were peaceful, that accepted and practiced peace. That is where he wanted them to operate from.

But in addition to this, another lesson also pokes through. The disciples were not supposed to bulldoze their way demanding things from the 'sheep'. They were not supposed to walk into the wealthiest and most comfortable homes and preach from there. They were not instructed to find the holiest or most righteous, the most well-known or as the Message translation puts it 'the best cook in town'. They were to seek 'the son of peace' (verse 6, KJV), wherever he was found. They were to look in the homes of widows, in two-parent homes, in the homes of the poor, in the homes of the devout. All the external trappings were not important. The socioeconomic status, the level of education, the marital status or the age of the homeowners didn't count. They were to look beyond the obvious, beyond the visible. They were to look for peace.

In these days of comfort and apparent affluence, we could do well to pray for discernment of what is inside people before we elevate them into positions of authority, before we entrust lives to them. We have to ask ourselves if we want them because they have the peace and the heart of Christ in them or because they cook great meals. It's hard to repair the damage caused by the fall of people from great heights. If we appoint people to positions of leadership without 'testing the spirit' (1 John 4:1) that operates in them then we reap the results of our rushed decisions when they reveal who they are and what is in them from a very visible position. This seems to be more evident in ministries that are growing faster than anointed leaders can be trained or identified. Sometimes we end up appointing people because they are there, or because they seem to have the heart to serve. There isn't enough time to train them adequately and when the going gets tough they crumble, from the platform, where everyone can see them.

I'm not being harsh in making this observation. I am speaking from personal experience. When a person is elevated into a pastoral position without some prior preparation, they can mess up not because they are a bad person but simply because they don't know what to do and it is very difficult to learn from a place of visibility with people you are supposed to be leading doing all they can to derail you because they don't want you there, you are too young, you are obviously ignorant, you are not from there, your efforts are judged at every turn. Because you did not have any prior preparation, you can destroy the very thing you are supposed to be building. You become bitter at the people who 'dumped' you in a place with ungrateful and critical congregants who preferred the status quo and oppose everything you do. But as you learn to trust God and as you realise that the work is his, you can then trust him to equip you for what he called you to do. This is grace at work, but I digress..

One more point that claimed my attention as I read Luke 10 is the fact that Jesus told his disciples to speak peace then wait and analyse the response they got. In these times where there is endless conversation on mobile phones, tablets, televisions and various forms of technology that do not give us any genuine listening time, it is easy to speak and act without allowing the crucial pause necessary for contemplation of the effects or impact of your words. But Christ told them to speak and then listen. This applies to our prayer life, to family relationships, to work situations and any scenario where there is supposed to be communication. We now need to be educated in the art of active listening. In other words we are being told to learn to 'shut up!'

The disciples needed to hear what was coming back to them in response to their greeting and their blessing of the home with peace. They couldn't assume that the house was peaceful just because it was quiet at that time. They needed to hear the 'son of peace' speaking peace back to them before they decided to stay and start impacting the community.

Although this might sound like over-kill on a couple of verses, I believe it is truth that could save us from a lot of regret. Whatever household we speak from becomes our testimony. If a household is full of peace and joy, love and respect for one another, these attributes will affect us, the inhabitants. To a point they will determine or affect our effectiveness. If we launch the ministry in a place full of strife then the strife simply multiplies as the ministry grows. If we launch from peace then that peace multiplies because we give to people what is in us, we sow into others what we have, just as much as we speak from the fullness of our hearts (Luke 6:45; Proverbs 4:23; Matthew 12:34). We can't set up camp in strife and expect to project peace and love.

One of the lessons I have learned in the last few years since I started attending the ministry God has placed me in is that I don't have the right to be offended or to take offence. Some lessons are hard to take in because they are like a sword that goes right to the core of who we are, the Word of God really is like a sword, a double edged sword (Hebrews 4:12). I think I used to take some warped sense of joy from being offended with people. I didn't think I even realised that I did that. I cancelled people from my life with ease. I didn't make any effort. You can imagine how that affects relationships. If someone said something I thought was silly I was out of there. But then the next person would also have a human moment and do something I didn't like and that was it, exit me! Now here were these men and women of God saying that I didn't have the right to take offense!

I think I was actually offended at them for taking away the power I had to end relationships and friendships, to never try to make things work. But now I am grateful for this lesson. It has made me realise that it is not all about me and that the same way other people give me a zillion chances, the same is also expected of me. Since I now operate from this place, my testimony has changed. There is no flippancy or superfluity in my relationships. I could not be effective in my father's house operating from a place of offense so that needed to be dealt with from the get go, and it was.

Peace. It is what Christ gave us, and it is what we also give. If it is at our core, in our homes, in our relationships and at work, we can reach out and be a blessing to those who are around us. Peace at home releases us to be generous and to genuinely impact lives. Drama and situations clamouring endlessly for our attention and time hinders our effectiveness. Peace releases, it does not bind or demand attention for itself.

There are some people that have a lot of drama in daily doses. Everything about them is a crisis. Their lives seem to be in perpetual crisis as if they are on a conveyer belt taking them from one calamity to another, from one catastrophe to another. If you spend a day with them you also end up becoming agitated because they expect you to partake of their drama. They drain you of joy and peace and impose their worry mode on you. I am wary of such people because they don't let you settle in the peace of God, they want to keep yanking you around from one type of drama to another and that is exhausting. Imagine being married to a panicker, Lord have mercy!

Jesus who is obviously very conversant with peace instructed his disciples to stay in the house they found peace instead of flitting around like butterflies from place to place. He encouraged stability, establishing some roots. Their light was to shine from that one place as the glory of The Lord rose and spread out into the community. People needed to know where they could find the disciples if they needed help, and it had to be a place soaked in peace enough that it oozed out to all around it.

I have learned in the last few years that peace does not necessarily mean that there are no challenges in one's life. Peace can pervade your whole existence while you are caring for a loved one who is graduating from this life to the next. Peace can be a constant companion for a single mother who is struggling to make ends meet. Just because she is a bit short of money is not a good enough reason for her to panic. She can trust God enough to rest in his reassurance, to allow his peace which surpasses all understanding (Philippians 4:7), peace that is at odds with how people think, to surround her and infuse her every day. Peace is how we as believers show that we trust our shepherd and know that he will lead us beside still waters and restore our souls (Psalm 23). Peace is a sign of trust in the God who promises not to leave or forsake us (Deuteronomy 31:6; Hebrews 13:5), the God who does not sleep or slumber (Psalm 121). Isaiah 26:3 reassures us that as we trust God, he keeps our minds in perfect peace. There is that link between trust and peace:

You will keep in perfect peace those whose minds are steadfast, because they trust in you

1 Corinthians 14:33 provides some insight into the nature of the God we serve:

For God is not a God of disorder but of peace--as in all the congregations of The Lord's people.

He is not a God of disorder, confusion, chaos, dissension or tumult. He is instead the God of peace. It is his nature and it is also his expectation of us as we claim to be as he is (1 John 4:17). We sometimes churn out verses and confessions without thinking about what they really mean. As he is so are we in this earth (1 John 4:17) means that we are love as he is love, we are people of peace as he is, we are truth as he is, we are good as he is. His nature is our nature so as he is a God of peace we too become people of peace not people of tumultuous or chaotic living.

I wonder how many of our children's lives would have turned out a lot better if we raised them in peaceful homes. How many of them would have spent more time with us, learning from us if we were more peaceful people with less strife and drama? Maybe the lack of peace in our homes has been the reason for our children's early exit, or our husband's leaving us, or our wives looking elsewhere? If someone thinks that living on the corner of the roof, exposed to the elements is better than living with you (Proverbs 21:9; 25:24) then maybe peace long departed from your relationship. There is so much strife that the corner of the roof looks really good.

Peace is part of the fruit of the spirit in us. As we allow the Holy Spirit not just to dwell in us but also to work in us, peace should be one of the evident results. The drama should lessen the more we let the Spirit of God work on us and in us. Fruit generally does not happen overnight. It is the final product of a process. I thank God we know what the fruit should contain, what it should be made up of. We can pray, we can analyse our lives, we can check our fruit to see if we are working hand in hand with the Holy Spirit or if the human aspects of us are still blatantly taking charge. If strife and jealousy are still a major part of us, then we may need to check what is wrong, we can't continue to yield the wrong fruit if the Holy Spirit is in us. The fruit he produces is described here:

But the fruit of the Spirit is love, joy, peace, longsuffering, gentleness, goodness, faith (Galatians 5:22)

My pastor has spent some time teaching from Mark 4, the parable of the sower. One of the statements he made which has stuck with me is that our hearts are the ground on which the Word of God, the seed is sown. The condition of that ground or soil determines the harvest. This does not just refer to the quantity of the harvest, I am sure it also applies to the quality of the harvest. It doesn't matter how good the seed is, if the ground is poor then the harvest is also going to be affected. A peaceful heart will yield different results from a restless and worried heart.

I come from a family of people who love growing things, we plant orchards, gardens, flowers and spend time working in the garden or the fields when we have the space to do so. My experience and observation is that sandy soils don't grow much on them, they are shifty and allow water to seep through and minerals and nutrients to be leached through. Clay soil on the other hand is compact. But it can also hinder plant growth as it becomes bogged, not letting water pass through it. As a result most crops die because there is too much water and not enough air circulation. The best type of soil appears to be the loam variety which is a combination of sand, silt and clay. This soil type retains some water and minerals and has better aeration than clay. Crops thrive more on it than the types mentioned before. The same applies to heart conditions. Some heart conditions don't allow anything to grow even though the Holy Spirit is present to help, they cannot yield peace or any other aspect of the fruit of the spirit. They hold on to grudges like clay not allowing anything to pass, they are like a stingy person who withholds more than they should and ends up with nothing (Proverbs 11:24). Or maybe they are like sand; they don't value the things they should so everything slips through their fingers. As a result they churn out strife, bitterness, jealousy, unforgiveness, chaos, hatred, rudeness, doubt and whatever is ideally grown in their type of heart condition.

I was taking a walk near a densely wooded area and I realised just how peaceful it was. The area across from it is residential and there is noise from people and cars. In the wood area the light was dim, everything looked calm and quiet. I would gladly have found a spot to sit and reflect because of the peace emanating from God's creation in those woods. It reminded me that generally, for me anyway I am most creative in a quiet and peaceful time and place without too much human interaction. I tend to write in the middle of the night when there is no sound from my neighbours, and if my children are at home they will be in bed. No one is likely to call me on the phone and there are no distractions. Those are the times I write or plan. They are peaceful times, creative times.

Human beings tend to bring what is inside them, whatever their heart is full of. We have a tendency to disrupt, we seem to find peace and quiet hard to handle, so there is music playing, the television is on, we chat needlessly and when there is no one to talk to we play drums on the table. But in that wooded area every sound appeared hushed and muted, there appeared to be a reverence of the surroundings.

God expects peace to be evident in our lives and in our speech. As we hear the Word of God and continue to grow from being babies to mature believers who can rightly divide the Word of truth (2 Timothy 2:15), as we learn to confess the Word, peace should emerge where we used to be strife-queens and kings. The Word (seed) won't change, but our hearts have to otherwise we continue to grow undesirable harvests.

There is an awesome promise to our children in Isaiah 5:13 which is that their peace will be great. God's desire for our offspring is that they will experience great peace. He sent out the 70 and told them to dwell where the son of peace also resided. They were to minister from a base that was filled with peace. He expects the same of us as we serve in his house, as we lead in whatever capacity. Our marriages, our families, our service, our businesses, must all be done and lived in peace. He is the Prince of Peace (Isaiah 9:16) and I am convinced that as he dwells with us he will bring more than just peace but the very essence of him which includes love, joy, excellence and every good and perfect gift which we know comes from him (James 1:17)

Isaiah 32:18 - _And my people shall dwell in a peaceable habitation, and in sure dwellings, and in quiet resting places_

5

David soaked it in praise

SOAK IT!

O magnify The Lord with me, and let us exalt his name together (Psalm 3:3 KJV).

David is one of those people I hope to sit down with in the sweet by and by and talk about the meaning of true praise and worship. It's not that he didn't face challenges. The man had enemies all around him and he was always at war with strange and familiar foe. Yet he isn't known for battle like Joshua. Nor is he known for despair like Job. We know him as the epitome of praise and worship.

How frustrating it must be for the enemy to try and floor someone, to throw issues at them from all directions yet this person composes songs of praise in the midst of what would drive most men mad. We don't always realise that if we respond to life in unexpected ways we confuse the enemy. If we laugh when people expect us to cry we confuse them, they think there is something wrong with us. But we don't have to behave in ways that are politically correct or acceptable. Our reaction should be based not on what we see but on what God says. I think as Christians we don't always realise the power of praise, the victory it unleashes and the spiritual dispersion of enemy forces and tactics that occurs when we praise and worship God in the midst of our trials.

Yet David seems to have grasped this fact and he praised God without inhibition. He praised God in contrast to human expectations, etiquette and decorum. He was a king but when it was praise and worship time he was able to set aside his position, his influence, his crown, his name and everything that separated him from the ordinary people around him. He didn't hold on to those things, he held on instead to the One who is the giver of all good and perfect gifts (James 1:17).

Pride is a horrible thing and I believe it is the reason why many people struggle with genuine worship. There are some worship leaders who can't worship. They are so full of their gifts they do all they can to focus people's attention on them, on their voices, on their actions, on what they are wearing. They forget that it is only as we lift Jesus up that he can draw all men unto him (John 12:32). If we want people to be impacted by our worship, then the worship has to stop being about us and more about God. Worship has to stop being a talent show to see who is the best, the most acknowledged and the most visible to being a time of directing people's attention, focus, thoughts and songs to Christ who alone can perfect their faith (Hebrews 12:2).

As I write this I am beginning to understand why David removed his kingly garments to worship, why he set aside his dignity to praise the Holy One of Israel (2 Samuel 6). You can't hold on to the trappings of human royalty and worship the King of kings. It has to be about him not you or anything else. Our eyes have to be focused on God and not on what is around us. Our minds have to be focused also on him and not on scheming and devising. We have to focus on what is important. The zeal for him, for his house, his goodness has to consume us (Psalm 69:9), has to take over and that can't happen if we are thinking about ourselves and how great we are.

In Revelation we read also about the elders removing their crowns as they worshiped God:

The twenty-four elders fall down before him who sits on the throne and worship him who lives for ever and ever. They lay their crowns before the throne and say ... (Revelation 4:10)

Then in 2 Samuel we get this account of the man after God's heart (1 Samuel 13:14; Acts 13:22) worshipping him:

Then David danced with all his might before The Lord. He had on a holy linen vest. David and all the Israelites shouted with joy and blew the trumpets as they brought the Ark of The Lord to the city. As the Ark of The Lord came into the city, Saul's daughter Michal looked out the window. When she saw David jumping and dancing in the presence of The Lord, she hated him (2 Samuel 6:14-16).

David danced with all his might. I can't even begin to picture what that means. In most churches people tend to sway rather than 'dance with all his might'. We tend to be self-conscious and dignified ever mindful of our positions, our clothes and even our neighbours. But David knew that he couldn't compete for space with the omnipotent and omnipresent God so he put everything important about his position aside and focused his eyes, his praise, his worship, on his God. This verse comes to mind:

He must become greater; I must become less (John 3:30).

If there are things that hinder our worship, things that compete with God for our praise and our worship, then we have to set them aside. Education has gone to the heads of many people. It has made them misunderstand rather than understand. It has left some so full of themselves that they have turned worship from God to themselves, from the Creator to their publications, from the Prince of Peace to their twisted theories and beliefs. But God won't share the platform with idols and with philosophers who are so twisted in their vision that they misplace themselves in the order of things, trying to push God out of his mercy seat, as if they could!

I have spent a lot of years in Universities and of late I realised that there seems to be a deliberate effort to discredit God or to make Christianity out to be a bad thing. I heard some lecturers discussing admission criteria and that there are certain people they wouldn't admit onto the social work course because of their Christian views but they have no problem admitting atheists and Muslims or people who very vocally and visibly portray their faith. My take on it is that they don't want to accept anything which shines brighter than them. They want all the credit to fall on them, their names to be scrolling in the credits of every achievement, every discovery, every dubious theory or current pedagogic trend. It's hard to acknowledge God if you think you are the bees knees.

I think that many men also struggle to bow before anything other than the things they can see and touch; the things they enjoy and the things in which their manhood is expressed. They can spend time watching sports but they are too busy to pray. They won't receive instructions from 'another man' and so they miss out on Godly counsel yet they can be led and guided by television.

This may be a generalization, but generally women seem to find it easier to praise and worship God. They seem to have less hang-ups about proving themselves and they seem to find it easier to yield to God. Maybe it is a testosterone thing, I don't know. But I know the impact it has on me whenever I see a man serving God sincerely, humbling himself setting aside his qualifications, his possessions, his place in society and giving himself up to serving his maker. There is something special and very attractive in seeing a man raise his hands and worship God, something beautiful in seeing a man sit at the feet of another because he is strong enough to realise that he needs to hear what God's servants are saying. He is confident enough in himself to know that listening to a pastor (male or female) does not make him less of a man. I think one of the most attractive things in a man is humility.

Having said that obviously there are some prideful women also who cannot yield to anyone or anything. Life has turned them into spiritually sinewy and tough warriors who wield verbal spears at anything that crosses their personal space. They question and fight with anything and anybody. They assume that if a man holds the door open for them he is despising them. They are little militant warriors.

My pastor preached on Joshua's attitude and this really helped me understand traits I used to have in my character because of my lived experiences. Even now I have to consciously submit to God's help because I grew up fighting for space. I had physical space but I felt like I had to fight for everything I needed. I felt like I was never heard and even my accomplishments seem to be inconsequential in my family, nobody seems to notice yet I am supposed to support everybody else's achievements. As a result I had to fight even just to be seen and noticed. That is how it appeared to me. And that is a Joshua spirit, a spirit of war! Joshua saw an angel and immediately drew his sword and challenged him (Joshua 5:13). He was used to fighting and having to deal with enemies all around him. As soon as he saw an unfamiliar person he had to work out if they were friend or foe. Life and its wars can turn you into a hard, unyielding person who is too proud to lift their hands and worship God because in lifting your hands you are surrendering whatever is already in them, you make yourself vulnerable.

Worship and praise are also about giving. They are about giving time, giving adoration, giving words, money, yourself, your possessions. Being able to release these things that are important to us is hard. Some people grew up with nothing, under difficult economic situations and they work hard to climb out of that pit. Asking them to give something they have worked hard for is like asking them to lose a limb. So any worship that involves giving materially becomes a real issue. Any worship that involves them also shedding their hard-earned status is also an issue. To justify the difficulty in parting with material things or to open up their homes, people then grumble and complain and share the views of the world. They have not learned that issues can be soaked in praise and worship. They have not learned that the same God who helped them out of poverty can keep them out of poverty and that as long as they are holding on so tight to their little accomplishments, they block out whatever new things God wants to drop into their hands.

When we read about Jericho and we hear about the exploits of Jehoshaphat or even when we see the Red Sea parted, someone praised God, spoke of the power of God, and worshiped him in whatever way God required. Whenever genuine praise and worship happens, walls crumble. When you start feeling really overwhelmed and you choose to praise God, things always shift and the heaviness lifts. Walls crumble. Life changes. David knew that and he spent time composing words of praise so that even for those among us who are not creative with words, we can still own David's catalogue of praise and we can worship our Father through David's psalms.

One of my favourite bible men is Asaph the son of Berekiah. Worship leaders could learn so much from this man who is also believed to have penned 12 Psalms (50, 73-83). Asaph and fellow musician Heman (a descendant of the prophet Samuel) were put in charge of the music in the house of The Lord (1 Chronicles 6). David knew the importance of music in praise and in worship so he had a group of Levites set aside for that aspect of the life of the Israelites. Asaph's descendants carried on the tradition and became musicians in God's house (2 Chronicles 35; Ezra 2:1).

In 2 Chronicles 21:30 King Hezekiah instructs the musicians to praise God 'with the words of David and of Asaph'. Asaph immortalised and perpetuated the words of praise that he wrote down not only for himself but for future generations.

What a blessing for us now! There are times when words don't come easily, but reading the Psalms can be an excellent way to pour out what is also in our hearts to the God of our salvation, and Asaph and David along with Moses and other current and past Psalmists have remained instrumental to a lot of praise and worship, they have remained at the core of our time of adoration of the Creator of the heavens and the earth (Genesis 1), the One who satisfies the longing soul and fills the hungry soul with goodness (Psalm 107:9).

Of course praise and worship are not just about singing and the prescribed praise and worship sessions in church. They encompass a wider array of actions, attitudes, and lifestyles. They are reflected in how we live and relate and also in how we serve God. Lives that are soaked in praise are full of awe and gratitude. They don't take anything for granted as if they have earned it or are owed it. They know their limitations and are quick to give credit to the One who gives them victory, life and strength, the One who has made them bold even in the face of challenges as he fills them with love, power and a sound mind (2 Timothy 1:7) which does not crumble at the approach of trouble. They are grateful and they express their gratitude to the God who walks through the valley of the shadow of death with them (Psalm 23) so that they have no need to fear because he is always there, never leaving, never forsaking (Hebrews 13:5; Joshua 1:5; Deuteronomy 31:6).

There are many illustrations of lives soaked in praise in the bible. We can usually identify them by how they responded to challenges, difficulties or miracles. Let's have a sneak peak at a couple of these people.

Mary was told that she was going to have a baby. She was a virgin. She had never done what naturally brings babies about. She was told that the laws of nature were not going to be followed this time; that her life was in effect just about to be turned upside down; she was being put straight into the lime light. Her reaction after the conversation with the angel ended was to visit Elizabeth and in Luke 1:46 – 55 to sing praises to the God who was causing this unusual situation to happen in her life. She didn't go to Elizabeth to gossip or grumble about her plans being disrupted, she knew that her cousin would help her work through things in a Godly way and both women soaked their situations in praise and in song.

There is an account of 10 lepers getting healed and sent on their way. Nine of them were happy to receive the healing and go their merry way. One of them though realised and appreciated the magnitude of the miracle he had experienced so he went back to give thanks and to worship the God of his healing. Because of that act of worship, more was added to what he had already received:

15 One of them, when he saw he was healed, came back, praising God in a loud voice. 16 He threw himself at Jesus' feet and thanked him—and he was a Samaritan. 17 Jesus asked, "Were not all ten cleansed? Where are the other nine? 18 Has no one returned to give praise to God except this foreigner?" 19 Then he said to him, "Rise and go; your faith has made you well (Luke 17).

The nine were cleansed as was the tenth leper. But because he returned to praise Jesus for what was done for him, he also received wholeness. His praise led to an intensity in the miracle he received so that it moved from just the physical cleansing to a total work of shalom, to spiritual, physical, emotional, relational and whatever else needed to be touched by the wholeness decreed by the King of kings. There are benefits to praise, it loosens things that have been tight and tightens those that were hanging loose.

This is how the Baker's Evangelical Dictionary of Biblical Theology defines 'praise':

Praise is the legitimate response to God's self-revelation. Personal experiences of God's deliverance and favor also elicit praise

As long as there is something God has done for us, we have a reason to praise. It might not be something 'big' according to the standards of the world but if he did it, we can praise him for it. As long as we have spiritual and physical eyes, we should be able to see what God is doing in our lives on a daily basis, and the more we see the more we will give him the glory.

I believe that lives that are bereft of praise are lives of people who are blind and so cannot see what God is doing. This has nothing to do with not seeing in the physical and a lot more with what I will term 'attitudes of blindness'.

Baker's Dictionary also makes these statements regarding praise:

To praise God is to call attention to his glory.

Whatever we are dealing with, if we focus on it, we can't focus on God. But if regardless of what we face each day, we focus on praising God, soaking our lives in praise, then the issues cannot remain huge or stifling because there is One that is higher and bigger than them, there is One that can flatten them. So we call attention to his glory not to the problems.

If you are alive that is something to praise God for, if you have wealth, health, family, children, a job, a home, you are saved, you have friends, you are married, you are single, if you are gifted, you are physically and emotionally whole, if you can read and have parents, if you are able to breathe unaided, if you don't live in famine or in a warzone, if you are free to come and go and are nobody's slave then you have a reason, you can praise God for whatever you are, have or do. You have a reason for soaking your life in praise.

6

Proverbs 31 woman soaked it in virtue

SOAK IT!

Proverbs 31 describes a woman who is the epitome of Christian womanhood. She represents the traits most men, Christian or not seek in a woman. I suppose it also represents traits many women would love to be their accolade. Whether or not there is any single woman who can tick every verse and claim it as her reality may be debatable, but these verses give us a template, a standard or a guideline to work from, pray with, believe about and praise God in as we see our lives changing to become more and more like the Word we have or should have hidden in our hearts (Psalm 119:11).

This set of verses used to upset me. They reminded me of what I was not; they highlighted my shortcomings, inabilities and inefficiencies. In fact they were used quite a bit by leaders, male and female to bash us over the heads and show how inadequate we were. At least that is the way it seemed to me and I know I may have misunderstood. I can only say what it felt like at the time and I really was puzzled by how

Proverbs 31 was quoted at us whenever we did not seem to meet an expected level of Christianity.

If a woman asked her husband for money to make a purchase she would have a few verses cited at her, letting her know that her lack of virtue contributed to her lack, and how if she was indeed a 'Proverbs 31 woman' she would not need to ask for money from her husband even if she worked full time and her earnings made up a chunk of the family income. I wondered why God would give fellow-believers, husbands and leaders ammunition with which to embarrass and shame those of us who were very human, those of us who had not yet attained whatever perfection we were supposed to achieve. But I thank God that Paul, that great man, apostle, teacher and author didn't pretend to be 'all that' and never made anyone feel like they didn't measure up. He was quick to state that he wasn't perfect and was working on some stuff like we all are:

Not that I have already obtained all this, or have already arrived at my goal, but I press on to take hold of that for which Christ Jesus took hold of me (Philippians 3:12)

Even though the woman portrayed in Proverbs 31 seems to exhibit unattainable traits, God knows we are not perfect and he has never judged us for our imperfections. He is not an unfair taskmaster who expects of us what he has not given us the ability to do. He is not like some parents who set such taxing and exacting standards that their children never have the hope to achieve and so they are criticised, compared to other people's children and made to feel inadequate. What God does instead is to give us the tools, the means, the strength and the grace to operate outside of and above our own best:

And God is able to bless you abundantly, so that in all things at all times, having all that you need, you will abound in every good work (2 Corinthians 9:8).

In Ephesians 1:8 we learn that God lavished on us not just this grace but also all wisdom and understanding. Equipped with these three (grace, wisdom and understanding), Proverbs 31 becomes my reality, becomes attainable. After all I can do all things through Christ who gives me strength (Philippians 4:13). Even though the bar has been set very high, the means to attain it are also high and of divine origin. I cannot be a 'Proverbs 31 woman' by myself, I can try and I can do my best but to really be the woman God expects me to be, the woman fulfilling the plans he has for me which will lead to my expected end (Jeremiah 29:11), I need grace, wisdom and understanding to be unleashed into my life. With them infusing my life, I can start ticking the Proverbs 31 boxes, I can change from whatever I am to a woman of virtue, a woman who can impact and affect her family, her community, her generation.

A woman who portrays the characteristics listed in Proverbs 31 is soaked in virtue and I know for a fact I want to be that woman. To better understand what it is we want to soak our lives in maybe a deeper comprehension of the term 'virtue' can be gleaned from words which are synonymous to it:

Goodness, righteousness, morality, uprightness, integrity, dignity, rectitude, honesty, honour, probity, propriety, decency, respectability, nobility, worth, good, purity, merit, respectability

Proverbs 31:10 begins with a question; it is not an assumption that the Proverbs 31 woman is a reality. The question suggests that maybe she is not easily seen, maybe she is not obvious in her virtuous self, maybe she doesn't know she is virtuous, maybe people around her don't realise that there is virtue in her, or maybe for the time being for whatever reason her virtue is hidden or submerged in whatever issues her life has thrown at her. In any case the author is presenting this woman's reality in question form.

He paints a picture of someone standing in the middle of a room looking for something. Just because it is not in his line of vision does not necessarily mean that it is not in the room. It may be buried under a pile of the papers on the table, the kids may have mistaken it for a toy and played around with it not realising the intrinsic value of it. Maybe this person thought they had put it in one place when it was actually in another. It appears to be lost but it might just be within arm's length. This person needs to make time to look for the item everywhere. He may have to unearth it from under a pile of stuff or he may need to shift some junk aside to get to it, he may have to crawl under a table or shine a light into a hidden corner. He needs to look and eventually his searching will be rewarded as he finds what he is searching for.

Even though the author of Proverbs 31 refers to us virtuous women by posing a question, this does not mean that the world is devoid of women of virtue. The virtuous women are there, they are virtuous but sometimes their loudness covers up the virtue and people leave them because they never get the chance to taste and see the virtue. Sometimes the pain from the past has helped them erect a fortress around their hearts so that no one can see past that to the wonderful woman inside. The virtue is there but lying dormant because no one can get to it to benefit from it. Pain, fear, low self-worth, lack of confidence, anger, bitterness, pride, hardness, a false sense of independence, foolishness and timidity can all cloak that virtue so that in the end it does not get the exposure it needs. As a result people ask if there is a virtuous woman and as a result people don't reap the benefits of living with a woman of virtue.

Why are we not meeting the virtuous woman everywhere we are, all around us? Possibly because her price is far above rubies, she is expensive (Proverbs 31:10). She is not a common occurrence, or a common sighting, she is not loud and brash. One has to look to see what is going on in her life to get a glimpse into her value. She is not shouting about her virtue from the top of the hills, yet at the same time her virtue is far-reaching in its impact as it affects her husband (Proverbs 31:11,23), her children (Proverbs 31:28), her workers (Proverbs 31:15), the travel industry (Proverbs 31:14), real estate (Proverbs 31:16), the business world (Proverbs 31:18, 24) the disadvantaged (Proverbs 31:20) and her community in general (Proverbs 31:23). Even though she doesn't purposely and purposefully draw attention to herself, attention has no option but to be drawn to her. The virtuous woman will emerge.

I find people to be very interesting subjects for study. The more I have consciously studied people the less heartache there has been in my life. I get to know people and this wealth of knowledge helps me relate with people who are totally different from each other without pulling my hair out because of some of the things they minor on and some of the superficial stuff they major on. I suppose there is virtue in each person but the difference is maybe how well secreted it is, how deeply it is embedded in their innards. Life would be easier if we all had x-ray vision so that as soon as we met people we could peel away the layers and immediately get to see what they are made of. Unfortunately life is not like that and more often than not we just have to relate by faith, hoping that at some point we will see something good in the people we relate with, similarly they also relate with us by faith.

One of the reasons some marriages and relationships fail is because it's too much hard work to get to the bits of a person that contain this virtue, the bit of goodness in them. For some life has been so harsh that it has scorched all the goodness and they have had to store it really deep within them. You try to work with such a person and they are brittle. They are fragile but they are also hard. You don't know what to say because they erupt at the slightest hint of criticism or at the slightest effort to see past their thick Jericho walls. The virtue is there but one has to ask about it because it is not easily accessible. In the end one has to decide if it is worth the effort it would take to get anything good out of the person. Unfortunately not everyone has the patience or the fortitude to persist in looking for virtue, so sometimes people just leave.

We can't allow what's good in us to be buried deep because of fear of being hurt. Life has an element of risk taking. People shouldn't have to be asking if there is a virtuous person when we are around. Our lives should be so soaked in virtue that it becomes evident at work, at church and at home. The bible talks about a woman who is married to an unsaved spouse and the fact that she can win him without words but just by her behavior, by evident virtue (1 Peter 3:1). I suppose this means that he can see the virtue in her and that is enough for him to want to remain married to her even though their faith walk is different. It is also enough to make him want to find out what makes her the woman she is. In the end he can also be saved, not because she preached *at* him, but because she became the salt that flavoured his life, the light in the areas of darkness around him:

Wives, in the same way submit yourselves to your own husbands so that, if any of them do not believe the word, they may be won over without words by the behavior of their wives

Colossians 4:6 refers to us all and not just to husbands and wives:

Let your conversation be always full of grace, seasoned with salt, so that you may know how to answer everyone

Proverbs 31:26 (KJV) continues this trend of thought:

She openeth her mouth with wisdom; and in her tongue is the law of kindness.

The virtue within us has to be visible and it has to impact and influence our families, our communities and the people who come in contact with us. It is not a secret weapon which we hide and keep under cover.

He said to them, "Do you bring in a lamp to put it under a bowl or a bed? Instead, don't you put it on its stand?

86

The virtue within us is a light-source from which people should get life, warmth and direction. People should never have to ask if there is a good person when we are there looking pretty but not exuding goodness and virtue.

There are people who don't just hide their virtue but have allowed it to be totally corroded and eroded. As a result their lives are soaked in such evil that there seems to be no remorse in them when they do wrong. They have acclimatised to the harshness of life and to the bad things they have experienced and instead of fighting, they have allowed it all to soak their lives leaving in their wake lives where virtue becomes a foreigner.

The wicked freely strut about when what is vile is honoured among men (Psalm 12:8)

There is a king called Jeroboam, son of Nebat who is mentioned in many passages in 2 Kings. In the same way that Kings who did what was right before The Lord were connected to David (1 Kings 15:11; 2 Chronicles 17:3), those who did what was evil were mentioned as basing their reign on the evil Jeroboam did. Just like the woman mentioned in Proverbs 31 symbolised virtue, Jeroboam symbolised evil.

What a legacy to leave for future generations of kings, to become the yardstick for evil rulership! Jeroboam so soaked his life in evil that it reached out into the future and tainted not only the future kings but also the kingdom in which they reigned and the flock they led.

Have a look at this:

After this thing Jeroboam didn't return from his evil way, but again made priests of the high places from among all the people. Whoever wanted to, he consecrated him, that there might be priests of the high places. This thing became sin to the house of Jeroboam, even to cut it off, and to destroy it from off the surface of the earth (1 Kings 13:33-34).

Nadab*: And he did evil in the sight of The Lord, and walked in the way of his father (Jeroboam) and in hi sin wherewith he made Israel sin (1Kings 15:26 KJV)*

Baasha: *He did that which was evil in the sight of Yahweh, and walked in the way of Jeroboam, and in his sin with which he made Israel to sin (1 Kings 15:34 KJV)*

Zimri: *because of the sins he had committed, doing evil in the eyes of The Lord and following the ways of Jeroboam and committing the same sin Jeroboam had caused Israel to commit (I Kings 16:19)*

Jehoahaz: *He did evil in the eyes of The Lord by following the sins of Jeroboam son of Nebat, which he had caused Israel to commit, and he did not turn away from them (2 Kings 13:2)*

There are many more citations of kings of Israel who did what was evil and followed the ways of Jeroboam. He and his namesake (2 Kings 14) who also became king and did what was evil in the sight of The Lord are mentioned nearly 100 times and most of the times refer to the evil they did as kings.

I believe that sometimes who a person is affects their environment. A nasty, harsh and hard person will repel good people who would have been helpful as iron sharpening whatever good may be in this person (Proverbs 27:17). But people can only take so much abuse before they move away and look for places where they can be nurtured rather than castigated for every little mistake. Soaking our lives in virtue, in goodness and strength makes us attractive and desirable. People are drawn to kindness just like moths are drawn to light. The iron fist can never win over a gentle caress. Let's allow the character of God to be our character. As he is, so are we, in this world (1 John 4:17).

As we soak our lives in virtue, we will impact the lives God has connected to us. People won't need to ask where the virtuous women are because they will see virtue in us.

7

Ethiopian Eunuch soaked it in the Word

SOAK IT!

Of late I have become both introspective and more aware of my environment. Not environment as in green issues which is important but environment as in what surrounds me, the people around me, the situations around me. I've started searching for the meanings of things happening in my life and as I have done so, I have also become increasingly appreciative of things that have previously appeared insignificant.

I particularly appreciate where I now am, not just in terms of physical location but more in terms of my spiritual journey. With age my sight is sharpening rather than dimming. Yes I wear spectacles, yes I may even have to extend things to arm's length to see them clearly sometimes but I can honestly say that I was blind but now I see (John 9:25). God is sharpening my vision and de-cluttering my view of my life, my dreams and the destiny and purpose he has assigned to my name. The things that used to take up a lot of my time no longer have the place of significance and it's a rather nice place to be.

Acts 8 talks about the Ethiopian eunuch who didn't see too well. He read but didn't get what he was reading. But the fact that he couldn't see didn't stop him reading. He decided to keep reading even while he was travelling. The Word of God was his reading material of choice. He soaked his life in it. He didn't scrub, he didn't paddle, he soaked his life in the Word which is able to change a life and which provides correction, reproof, instruction, doctrine and perfection (2 Timothy 3:16), which is sharper than a two-edged sword and which can separate the nitty-gritty of each issue (Hebrews 4:12). He didn't soak once nor did he soak briefly. He just soaked not knowing when the softness would come or when the grease would break down.

This man makes me think of the verse in Ecclesiastes 11:1 and 11:4. We are encouraged to cast our bread on the waters and that we would find it after many days, also that we are to sow even if the conditions don't look ideal. We are to sow the Word of God also in our hearts even when it makes no sense. As people of faith we don't wait for perfect conditions. We sow whether it is raining or scorching hot. In the same way that God sent Philip to talk to the Ethiopian and help him get understanding of the Word, he will also send someone who will teach and bring us the understanding we need or he will reveal his word to us in whatever way he wants to use. Our task is to faithfully sow in expectation.

In a way the Ethiopian also reminds me of Naaman (2 Kings 5) who was told to dip himself in the Jordan seven times. Had he dipped just the one time he wouldn't have got his total healing. He had to do it over and over until he got healed. Another example is in 2 Kings 13 when Elisha asked Jehoash to shoot an arrow through the window. Jehoash obeyed but only so much. He didn't soak, he dipped and removed it. He only shot the arrows three times leading to Elisha's anger as he asked him why he had stopped instead of shooting again and again. He limited the holy one of Israel (Psalm 78:41), he didn't give the issues in his kingdom time to soak in the Word of God. He went for the quick response which had neither depth nor longevity. As a result his victory over his enemy was short-lived.

What causes me to stop and reflect on the two case studies above is the fact that the outcome is determined to a great extent by us. God is present to heal, to help, to deliver and all that. But a lot depends on our availability and on our involvement, on how much access we give God, his word, the

Holy Spirit into whatever it is we are dealing with. If we confess weakness and illness, if we take possession of genetic and other conditions we allow them a stronger hold in our lives than if we soak them in the Word of God. Our attitude is important, as is our confession of what we have hidden and stored in our hearts (Psalm 119:11). We determine the outcome by what we say.

If we marinate a piece of meat for 10 minutes, we get a 10 minute result. If we marinate it overnight, we also get a difference in the depth of the flavour and the impact on the tenderness of the meat. If we do mini word soaks then we can't expect major results. We have to be serious about marinating and basting our lives with the Word of God. As we do so we will see the impact and the effectiveness of the Word in dissolving and degreasing, in loosening and cleaning. God in his wisdom knew that we needed this ongoing marination in his word and so he reminds us not to neglect the times of coming together and being fed the Word (Hebrews 10:25). He knows our frailty (Psalm 103:14) and that we easily forget when the going gets tough so we need to be in a place where we continue to hear the Word, to read the Word and to confess the Word so that we can see the results he has planned for us.

The Ethiopian did what the children of Israel were told to do in Deuteronomy 11:18:

Fix these words of mine in your hearts and minds; tie them as symbols on your hands and bind them on your foreheads

He obeyed Joshua who encouraged the children of Israel to keep the 'book of the law' before them always, not to allow it to depart from their sight but to meditate on it day and night (Joshua 1:8). He kept at it in season and out of season, at home and on the road. And as he kept on reading, God provided Phillip to explain, clarify, reveal and bring understanding to this eunuch. Had he read once and set the book aside because he didn't understand, God wouldn't have had to send someone to help him. But he soaked and kept soaking his life in the Word, and God who sees the heart had to send him help from the sanctuary (1 Samuel 16:7; Psalm 20:2).

This brings to mind the scripture about the zeal for God's house consuming us (Psalm 69:9). If we are zealous for the things of God I know God brings wisdom and understand, he brings us help. He won't leave us to flounder more so in things concerning his house, his name and his word. If we turn up, if we are zealous, if our motives and desires are towards him he will bring us the help we need. He will bring us to our own Elizabeth who will cause the baby in us, the gifts, the calling, the talents, the virtue to stir and spill out into unexpected expressions (Luke 1:39-). He will bring us alongside our own Johns who will call people's attention to us. God will align our paths with our Elijas who will leave us their cloak and anoint us for our double portion of ability and service (2 Kings 2:14).

More and more I am now learning the power of agreeing with the Word of God rather than with the circumstances around me. I am finally mastering the art of speaking right, speaking the Word, rejecting the cultural and the academic voice, the socially accepted opinion and what may even be the popular trend of speech. My life has turned around because more and more I have learned to apply the Word to each issue and situation. Even when I am afraid, when the circumstances seem to be bigger than me or my faith appears inadequate, I am speaking what the Word says and the more I speak it the more I decree and declare it, the less intimidating the situations become and the more I see God arise and my enemy get scattered (Psalm 68:1).

I was just thinking the other day about the impact of traditions and culture on a Christian. Culture has a peculiar language that it speaks. Sometimes its vocabulary agrees with God's Word but there are times when it is in direct contrast to the Word. A person has to decide which voice they give precedence and credence to particularly so in their decision-making processes. If there is ever a conflict, the Word of God has to have final authority. Everything else has to bow.

I was thinking about my mother some time ago and I realised that even though she was a prayerful woman, a strong Christian as some might say, I also know that she was sometimes conflicted in her faith. Because of her upbringing, it was difficult for her to always silence the traditions and the culture, the family voice. I notice this in her generation. They were steeped in some practices and traditions, practices of worship that are in direct contrast with the Word of God, but they are also the generation that received the Gospel when it was preached to them. So even though they received Christ or church membership and for some, some kind of religion, they also equally held on to what had been drummed into them by their parents, grandparents and community and it is not easy to relinquish the hold of those things. So sometimes my mother would refer to how things were done and I would ask her what scripture substantiated her stance. But I thank God that because she was yielded to the Holy Spirit she prayed through every situation and more and more her confessions lined up with the Word of God.

I am grateful for my upbringing. People don't always realise how hard it is to un-teach someone things they were taught from birth. That is why sometimes people want to go to a church where people 'understand them'. They want to be Christians but they also want to still follow some of their cultural beliefs. They want to be with people who do things the same way they do. That can be a spiritually dangerous place to be because in the end culture simply takes over, it is being practiced in a church but it is the main voice that is listened to. People don't always realise that in some ways this is idol worship, it is exalting something above God, it is believing a report that is not of or from God. But I thank God that as much as they could, my parents taught us the Word of God. They took us to church and in all my life, I never saw them expressing belief in anyone besides God himself, Christ and him crucified   (1 Corinthians 2:2). We grew up 'ignorant' of what other families did, in fact we read a lot of things in books but never experienced them in our lives and for that I am truly grateful to my parents and my paternal family.

It takes courage, determination and stubbornness to speak the Word when everything around you is falling apart. In a way it is a form of going against the grain. But agreeing with the issues you are facing does not solve them. Soaking your pain in tears does not diminish it. The only thing that will shift debt, poverty, sickness, hunger, sin, foolishness, addictions and everything else that might be encrusting your life is the Word of God. The Word has to be read and heard, it has to be confessed and believed. When this hearing and speaking and confessing is repeated (Romans 10:17) then things change. All the tears in the world won't heal cancer or end poverty. All the pity parties in the world won't cause an errant spouse to come to his or her senses. Only the Word of God has the power to change things, to cause situations to turn around. Only the Word has already been assigned to change your life and it is on a mission from which it cannot return without accomplishing what it was sent to do (Isaiah 55:11).

I love the Hebrews 12:1 scripture which talks about the great cloud of witnesses. For me it refers to the people that have gone before us but whose lives have been laid bare for us to dissect and learn from them. In a way they are like the people who donate their bodies for science. We can study muscles and tissues, cells and systems from actual bodies of people who lived then passed on. The biblical bodies we can learn from are the Ruths, the Davids, the Jobs and Marys, the Joannas, the Achsahs and the Sheerahs. They each have things they can teach us posthumously. A lot of them didn't speak in line with the Word. Many of them after being used by God greatly still didn't soak their lives with the Word or with the right confessions. Some of them have become crucial examples of how not to speak!

Think about Jonah after his message led to the people of Niniveh and their king repenting and God forgiving them. Jonah was angry and wanted to die. He threw a major tantrum because he wanted God's destruction on those people. Even though he said these words, he didn't seem to believe or understand their impact just like the Ethiopian eunuch who read but didn't understand:

He prayed to The Lord, "Isn't this what I said, Lord, when I was still at home? That is what I tried to forestall by fleeing to Tarshish. I knew that you are a gracious and compassionate God, slow to anger and abounding in love, a God who relents from sending calamity (Jonah 4:2).

An even better illustration is the well-known and revered prophet Elijah who was an awesome prophet. But when Jezebel threatened him he not only ran away but seemed to forget who he was. All the victories God had just given him were forgotten. He soaked his life in fear, not fear of The Lord but the fear of man, the fear of a woman and his confession showed this in 1 Kings 19:4b:

He came to a broom bush, sat down under it and prayed that he might die. "I have had enough, LORD," he said. "Take my life; I am no better than my ancestors."

In the heat of the moment this man who had called fire down from heaven and done wonders demonstrating the power of his God, forgot all that and started agreeing with the situation he was in. It feels like such a let-down for us because we know what a mighty man he was, but at the same time I suppose it is a lesson for us, that it is easy to revert to common talk and forget to tune in to the uncommon, the unmatchable and incorruptible word of the Most High. Elijah wasn't the first and he won't be the last believer to allow fear to take over for a while, but as long as he remains one of our huge cloud of witnesses, we will continue to be reminded that our lives, our words, our confessions and conversations all need to be soaked and steeped in the living word of God.

Keeping in mind what John 1 says about the Word, we know the Word is Christ:

In the beginning was the Word, and the Word was with God, and the Word was God. He was in the beginning with God. All things came into being through Him, and apart from Him nothing came into being that has come into being ……….. and the Word was made flesh, and dwelt among us...

Keeping also in mind that at the mention of the name of Jesus every knee shall bow, we have to make sure the traditional and cultural voices bow, curtsy and surrender pride of place when Jesus speaks:

That at the name of Jesus every knee should bow, in heaven and on earth and under the earth (Philippians 2:10; Romans 14:11)

8

Woman with Alabaster box soaked in sacrificial giving

SOAK IT!

I think whenever genuine giving happens there are people who get upset, the enemy gets really angry. I suppose this anger is on two fronts:

> ➢ Sacrificial giving makes a genuine difference and impact to the recipient
> ➢ The sacrificial giver receives appropriate harvests

Both the giver and the recipient benefit from it. Sometimes people around a genuine giver also get upset because the bar is being raised and they don't want to give to the same extent, so they get upset and they ridicule the giver.

People like comfort and sometimes sameness is safe. They don't always want to change because change usually involves doing; it requires some expending of energy. So if you start giving more people don't want you to because then you show up their minimal giving.

The woman with the alabaster box gave like Abel. Their giving caused those who were not genuine in their service to grumble and murmur. In fact their giving showed just how little everyone else was giving. Imagine a scenario where the best sprinter in a nation goes to the Olympics and comes last in a race. He may be running fast but his true ability is challenged when pitted against those doing a better job. He may have been patting himself on the shoulder because in the area he lives he is the best but when better sprinters come alongside him, he realises just how limited his speed is. He is not likely to smile at that. If he wants recognition then he has to work harder to catch up; he has to train harder and sacrifice time, sleep and sometimes food.

In Matthew 26:7-9 the disciples were indignant at the 'waste' or extravagance they saw when the woman poured expensive perfume on Jesus' feet. They had very good ideas on how the perfume could have been better used. It wasn't their perfume, they didn't contribute to its purchase, but they had an opinion about how it should have been used.

But between verses 10 and 13 Christ puts this woman's giving in perspective:

He commended the giver. The bible says that it is more blessed to give than to receive (Psalm 41:1) and as this woman was giving, Christ acknowledged her gift as a 'beautiful thing' (v 10).

Jesus then put a season to the gift. It was appropriate that this woman gave this gift while he was still there with them. It was a timely gift, given at the right time to the right person (v 11). It wasn't a careless gift just thrown out there because it is our custom to give. Instead it was well thought out and planned and it was given to the right person at the right time. It was like a corn seed planted in well-aerated compost-rich soil just before the onset of heavy rain.

Jesus then did something I find really special. He gave meaning to the seed or the gift. He didn't receive it carelessly but linked it to his own life and death, to one of the most important events ever to happen on this earth and I suppose in heaven as well. He helped his hearers understand the revelation regarding seeds, sowing and giving. In other words in verse 12 our Lord tells this generous woman that her seed has eternal significance. No wonder the enemy's hackles were raised.

In verse 13 Christ decreed longevity to the woman and her act of giving. He put his seal of approval on what she did and opened the door to her being part of the gospel, the good news that would traverse the world from place to place, generation to generation.

This woman's seed was recorded for eternity. I wonder what sort of impact our seed has. Are we so much as scratching the surface or are we giving carelessly, seed that cannot be ascribed eternal or even lingering value?

Another generous giver is a man called Abel. He gave his best. He gave from the firstborn of his flock (Genesis 4:4) but his brother Cain brought some of the fruit of the soil as his seed (Genesis 4:3). Cain's seed seemed generic, nothing personal whereas Abel's seed was specific, targeted, from what he owned, what was his, what he had spent time on, it was a seed that took something from him. In a way Abel gave of himself whereas it would appear his brother just gave what he could get hold of. Abel's gift was received but his brother's was not. Cain was angry, murderous rage consumed him till he killed his brother. He didn't realise that he couldn't silence a giver (Hebrews 11:4), and Abel, like the woman with the alabaster box is still a role model for any of us who want to give genuinely, meaningfully and with impact, he has not been silenced but still speaks to this day (Hebrews 12:24).

I would say that the woman with the alabaster box gave extravagantly. She went beyond ordinary giving to giving lavishly, unreservedly, exorbitantly and generously. Her seed was purposeful; she soaked it in sacrificial giving. The widow with the two mites did the same (Luke 21; Mark 12). From these two women we get lessons on giving:

➢ Giving proportionately to what we get
➢ Realising that God does not focus on the amount but on the heart
➢ God takes notice of giving that is sacrificial and sincere (Mark 12:44; Luke 21:4)

These people all teach us about giving that is sacrificial, purposeful, targeted and honourable. They had no Ananias and Sapphira motives (Acts 5). They soaked the issues in their lives in giving that was sincere and as a result, they were acknowledged by the One who can stretch and multiply what we put in his hands (Matthew 14; Mark 8; Luke 9; John 6; Mark 6; John 9).

It's hard to narrow down the field of givers because the bible is packed with wonderful witnesses in this area, people who were prepared to go the extra mile, people like the widow of Zarephath who gave the very last meal she had, even though she had a hungry child (1 Kings 17). She did not eat her seed but sowed it and was fed and provided for, for the rest of her life. Had she eaten that last meal she would have died. But instead, she gave sacrificially and reaped exceedingly and abundantly beyond anything she could think or ask (Ephesians 3:20).

Hannah also gave sacrificially and reaped more than she gave. She pledged to give her son to The Lord (1 Samuel 1:11). He gave her a son and she kept her vow and took him to the house of The Lord (1 Samuel 1:28). The barren woman gave a womb-opening offering and in place of the one child she gave, she got five more (1 Samuel 2:21).

Hannah gave in faith. She didn't wait until she had a child to prepare her seed. Even before she got pregnant she was already sowing her seed. She was allowing God to use her womb to bring a mighty prophet into the world. She gave what she wanted and hungered for most, the one thing she was praying for she was also willing to give. She didn't hold on to her motherhood just like Christ did not hold on to the fact that he was God. He set that aside for our sake, because he knew the power of the seed he was about to sow:

Who, being in very nature God, did not consider equality with God something to be used to his own advantage; rather, he made himself nothing by taking the very nature of a servant, being made in human likeness (Philippians 2:6-7).

Isaac is another great example of soaking our situations in giving, effective giving. He sowed in times of drought and reaped a hundred fold (Genesis 26:12). Isaac didn't wait for the time when everything was balancing out and there was surplus. He sowed at a time when there appeared as if the seed could not possibly yield fruit or a meaningful harvest. He did not focus on the weather or the amount of moisture present. He followed the truth of the Word that seed time is followed by harvest (Genesis 8:22) and so he sowed.

What super harvests we could enjoy if only we stopped calculating precipitation; (*Whoever watches the wind will not plant; whoever looks at the clouds will not reap Ecclesiastes 11:4*). If we just obeyed the Word and went ahead and sowed even in the times when we have little. As we give, it is given back to us, not the same thing we give but yes according to the measure with which we give and also multiplied back to us in good measure, pressed down, shaken together and overflowing onto those people around us (Luke 6:38).

Of course the best example of sacrificial, purposeful, targeted and extravagant giving is our Heavenly Father. He soaked the issue of our redemption, the need we all had for salvation in sacrificial giving, giving his own son. He gave for people who didn't ask him to and many who will still not acknowledge what he did. He gave for people who didn't even know they needed a saviour and for those who mocked and still mock him for it. Christ gave his own life and now he can see the travail of his spirit and he is glad (Isaiah 53:11). He is reaping each time someone turns to The Lord. He is seeing the harvest of the one seed that he gave; his own life.

The target of his sacrifice remains the people he created and loves. He gave more than what anybody else could even though he didn't have to. His sacrifice remains unmatchable. He purposed in his heart that he would give the best gift possible, he lay his own life down (John 15:13) so that we could once again have hope, so that we could live where we had been destined to die. He didn't have to keep giving that gift. His heavenly father accepted it and acknowledged it for posterity. So now as long as we accept him, we are saved, we have been given power to become children of God (John 1:12).

Good parents give sacrificially to their children. Some mothers have even given their lives at birth to bring a child into the family. Women have surgery to ensure the safe delivery of their children. They go through one of the most painful ordeals as they push their baby out. They sacrifice their bodies, their health, their time and everything they have to give their children whatever they need. Good fathers shelve their dreams to make sure they provide for their families. They give sacrificially and are sometimes rewarded as they see their offspring thriving and excelling. Sometimes their gift is mocked by ungrateful children who forget what their parents went through to give them the opportunities they received.

We have a choice in our giving, not just the giving of offerings and tithes, but in our giving of love, time, comfort, and anything else we can sow in God's house and in the lives of the people around us. We can do a Cain type of giving or we can soak our lives in alabaster box type of giving. It is not wasted, our seed lives and multiplies. But it has to be given, it has to be surrendered so that the multiplier can multiply it, so that The Lord of the harvest (Matthew 9:38) can give it a body and cause it to increase.

Our seed returns to us in good measure, pressed down, shaken together and running over (Luke 6:38). I've noticed of late on social networks how people are doing their best to discourage believers from giving and from tithing. They are posting discouraging comments which would easily sway someone from giving or tithing. But giving and tithing, the sowing of whatever type of seed we put in the ground are personal issues that we decide based on the Word of God, our love for God and our need for a harvest. If we decide to accept and follow the new-fangled thought patterns, ideologies and doctrines; that is a choice with consequences we also have to live with.

Even if God did not promise the good measure and the harvest from our seed, I would still give because of what giving does to me, for me and in me. I would give to see the impact of my giving, to see the smile on the face of someone I have blessed, to know that I have given and done something which is more blessed than what happens when I receive (Acts 20:35). There is power in giving.

It really is more blessed to give than to receive (Acts 20:35). To give means that God has blessed you enough to have something you can share with another. Soak your life in giving, in reaching out to impact the lives of your family, friends, neighbours and community. Keep in mind that giving is not just about money but about love, kindness, time, friendship and of course material things.

9

Woman with the issue of blood soaked it in faith

SOAK IT!

When you have a forked path in front of you, then you have the luxury of choice. You can choose to walk down path A, B, or C. You don't have to focus on any one of them as they present you with alternative routes to where you want to go. You don't have to express serious loyalty to any one of the routes because should one prove to be too bumpy you still have two more to use and still get where you are headed. A believer who has plan A, B and C for their life does not really need to have strong or growing faith in God. They have too many alternative support systems. If one fails they try the other and then the other as well. They have alternatives, options and choices.

The woman with the issue of blood had got to that point in her life where she had traipsed along every imaginable path. She had seen the doctors and all the other people who could have healed her. Plans A, B and C had all been exhausted and she now came to the point in her life where there were no more forks in her road. She had nowhere else to go and she had nowhere else to look except up. The luxury of choice had been used up. Her issue was still as tough as it had been before she went looking for help in all the places she went to. Nothing had helped. She now had to find the only thing in which she could soak her health issue. She realised that her only option was faith.

I had a health situation that was escalating not only in pain and discomfort but also in its impact on my life as a whole. It was affecting my ability to do day to day stuff like sitting or sleeping, driving or standing up. Nothing I did was comfortable and there were times when tears streamed down my face unchecked. I was in agony and there did not seem to be any solution to it. Doctors gave a lot of advice and pain killers that didn't work. It got so bad that I didn't know what to do. But I also knew that I couldn't carry on as I was. In all the time I was going through this I had a forked path in front of me. I had options. I had my GP, my packs of pain medication. I had the option to see a specialist and of course there was the internet churning out useful and useless information about the issue. A time came when I had seen the specialists, followed all advice, used various medicines but I realised that things were not getting any better. Finally I did what I should have done at the beginning. I went into my bedroom and prayed for healing. By the following day I was back at work without pain and I kept walking gingerly in case the pain returned but it didn't. I could have saved myself a lot of pain had I soaked that whole issue in a prayer of faith, but I had too many options at that time. I still find myself testing myself or anticipating pain because it seems strange to be pain-free after being in pain for so long. But God honoured those few minutes of faith expressed through prayer and I have been healed for more than five years.

I think sometimes women find themselves in a situation where they stay in relationships because they have made the man to be their option and the answer to all their needs and issues. They have soaked their whole life in a person. As a result the man can treat them whichever way he wants and they will not leave. Once that option is snatched away through divorce or when abuse becomes unbearable then they start thinking back and reminiscing about their Sunday school days, the verses they used to memorise and the songs they used to sing on their grandmother's lap. Only when the man option, the status option and all the other paths they were relying on have shut down then they go back to the real Way (John 14:6) who is also their shepherd and who is able to lead them into the green pastures they so desire (Psalm 23).

I suppose it's not surprising that sometimes people come to church when they are desperate and when they have 'run out of options'. They only use God as their last resort, when everything else has been tried, when every road has been walked on till it is dry. What is the point in suffering first and being damaged first before coming to the place you should have been in the first place? I wish I had come to my father's house sooner and avoided all the hell I have gone through in my life. I could have avoided so many pitfalls I have periodically fallen into. Financially, relationally, emotionally and even in issues to do with my career, I should have come to God first before allowing people to direct my path. I should have blocked and blanked out every alternative, every plan B that has wasted so much of my time as I explored dead ends relationally, financially and in just about every area of my life.

Christ tells us that he is the Alpha and Omega (Revelation 22:13). He is the beginning and the end and I am sure he is also or wants to be to us everything in between. I love the scripture which says that my walls are continually before him (Isaiah 49:16). He wants me to be in a place of advantage where I am like a child who is playing in the back yard under mummy's watchful eyes. Unfortunately most of us won't stay in that place where underneath are the everlasting arms (Deuteronomy 33:27), surrounding us guiding, guarding and protecting while comforting and shielding. Oh no, we find that too restrictive! We want to do our own thing so we escape and go try out whatever religious, financial, relational paths we are curious about and come back hurt, broken and abused. But our God still stretches out his arms to us and calls out:

Come to me, all you who are weary and burdened, and I will give you rest (Matthew 11:28).

In Luke 5 19-20 two friends can't get to Jesus because there is a crowd around him. They don't have a plan B for their friend. They know that the healing their friend requires can only be found in the man from Galilee.

They could have waited until the crowd thinned. Or they could have given up and gone back home, realised that their attempts to get to Christ were futile. But these guys knew that things soaked in faith were loosened. Nothing remained hard and tough when faith was applied, the impossible became possible. So they decided to do the unconventional. They decided to get to Christ by any means possible even if they had to create an entrance through the roof and this is how the saviour responded to them:

When Jesus saw their faith, he said, 'Friend, your sins are forgiven'

He saw their faith, it soaked their love, their persistence, their actions. In addition to the healing this man needed, he also got forgiveness for his sins.

When I look back at my life particularly so in the last ten years I am amazed at some of the decisions I have made. I was not a particularly brave person and growing up I was well known in our family for being extremely fearful. I was always second guessing myself and even now this is something I have to keep an eye on as it tends to try and creep back into the life it was banished from. But my life got to the point where I needed to make some tough decisions and up to now I sometimes wonder where the courage came from. But I believe the scriptures when they tell us that even a little bit of faith can move mountains (Matthew 17:20; Luke 17:6). Human beings focus more on quantity than quality. But God can move if a little part of me is reaching out to him. I just need to remember that I am not the one that will move the mountain. The faith is not in me or my abilities. It is faith in God and in what he can and will do.

It would appear then that I must have had that mustard seed size faith because I certainly didn't feel like a person full of faith. But I stepped out into totally unfamiliar territory with nothing to fall back on. I moved to a new country thousands of miles from home. I did a major relocation with four children to a job in a town where I knew nobody. After working in secure employment for five years I trekked my travel weary children hundreds of miles to a new place with no tangible prospects. But God has continued to honour each step of faith, he has continued to open doors, to provide, protect and sustain us in a foreign land. I don't think I always consciously sprinkled faith on my issues. I think sometimes life can bring you to a place where you reach out in faith without thinking about it anymore. Faith becomes your automatic response to challenges and life. I really wouldn't want to be anywhere else. Faith is an awesome grease-buster!

The woman who was healed from the issue of blood must have debated with herself in trying to map out a course of action. She knew that she wasn't supposed to be in the crowd since she was considered to be unclean. She was a woman trying to push through a crowd probably dominated by men. She was ill. She knew that Christ could heal her. She needed to exercise her faith because it was directing her to the place of her deliverance. She pushed through trying to be inconspicuous, allowing only the faith in her heart to strengthen her enough to touch just the hem of his garment then step back healed.

Just thinking about this awesome woman makes me realise that it is not always easy to get to the place where our healing, blessing or help is. There is always a throng around it. There is fear sometimes, pain, insecurity and self-doubt. Sometimes pride stops us from seeing what should be ours or words that have been spoken which we have foolishly allowed to enter our hearts can form an impenetrable wall that blocks our line of blessing. But if we soak it all in faith like the woman with the issue of blood, the crowd is inconsequential, what matters is the fact that we can push through by faith and get to our site of deliverance and wholeness.

Many of us expect bells to toll when we have a testimony. We want our faith to be rewarded by recognition, in which case we are snatching the glory from God to ourselves. But this precious woman did not want any fanfare. She just wanted to be healed and she had the faith that moves mountains.

In a prayer line sometimes it is easy to see those who are soaking their issues in faith. They come to God in faith not to people. While some people are standing around observing what is going on, those operating in faith are receiving even before they are prayed for. They are already reaching out to touch the hem of his garment. They recognise the fact that God is their healer and that he uses his servants in fulfilment of this promise in Mark 16:17-18:

And these signs will accompany those who believe: In my name they will drive out demons; they will speak in new tongues; they will pick up snakes with their hands; and when they drink deadly poison, it will not hurt them at all; they will place their hands on sick people, and they will get well.

So when they go forward to be prayed for they do so in faith. They don't look up to see who is praying for them but they receive what they know that God is doing for them, by faith.

It's not possible to talk about faith without referring to Hannah or to the heroes mentioned in Hebrews 11. That is a true Hall of Faith which introduces us to a collection of imperfect human beings who despite their shortcomings chose to have faith, to soak their issues, challenges and families in faith. They trusted God when it was not fashionable to do so, when no one else did, when their positions could have detracted from their walk of faith and when there did not seem to be any possibility that what they wanted could become a possibility. There is no need to reinvent the wheel. We can use Hebrews 11 and learn from this collection of people who are not really that different from us.

We don't even have to look at people but at God himself. He created tangible things by speaking, sending his word out to create. In reading about creation in Genesis 1, we get a lesson on how God wants us to live. Since we believe that we are as he is in this earth (1 John 4:17), that means we also do what he does. He created by faith, by releasing his word, by speaking to the thing that he wanted to happen and bringing it from where it couldn't be seen, translating and transferring it by his word from invisible to visible, from chaos to order. That is what our life-style also ought to be since we are also created in his image (Genesis 1).

Then there were people like Abel, Enoch, Noah, Abraham and Sarah who defied natural laws and did what couldn't normally be done at their age. Then came their progeny, Isaac, Jacob, Joseph, Moses and the generation that shouted the walls of Jericho down. These all soaked their lives in faith. They believed God and they stepped out in faith.

Other soakers in faith followed: Rahab, Gideon, Barak, Samson, Jephthae, David, Samuel. There were many whose names are not mentioned but who also soaked their life issues and responded to them in faith, overcoming serious hurdles and seeing miracles as their lives were turned round. Faith is what we live by (Habakkuk 2:4; Hebrews 10:38), it is a powerful connector to our source of life, health, wealth and genuine shalom.

So next time trouble comes, don't respond in fear, respond in faith. Even if you don't know what to do, trust that the Creator God does know. Know that he can solve what appears to be unsolvable.

10

Prophet's widow soaked it in obedience

SOAK IT!

Anyone who has raised teenage children will tell you that sometimes parents feel as if they are locking horns with strangers in their homes. They challenge anything the parents say and sometimes push boundaries all the way into prison, or into some mistake which ruins their lives. In a way a parent can feel as if they have lost their pliable, obedient child and replaced them with a rebellious stranger. Nothing the parents say is accepted at face value anymore but is analysed, questioned, challenged and often disregarded and discarded. It can be a tough time for parents and for the kids as well.

Obedience is tested in any relationship that is tiered. Employees test their employers, spouses vie for authority and power, children challenge their parents' authority and the body of Christ sometimes struggles to obey the husband of the church, the one who loved them enough to lay down his life (John 15:13; John 10:18; 1 John 3:16). In schools teachers seem to wrestle with their students for authority and many students delight in discomfiting their teachers and disobeying their instructions. We seem to intrinsically have a penchant for trying to pull down anyone who has any form of step on a higher rung than we are on the ladders we find ourselves. I'm not sure why we think a flat line is more acceptable than a rugged upward graph where we can all keep going up a step as we attain parental, professional, spiritual or financial authority. We seem to be more comfortable if everyone stays the same, no one makes more progress than those around them regardless of the investment each puts into their life.

But there are so many cases we read about of people that have demonstrated that obedience really is better than sacrifice (1 Samuel 15:22). They have obeyed God even when they didn't understand why they needed to obey or what benefit there was in obedience. They obeyed when the expectation for them to obey seemed to be unreasonable.

As we have become increasingly 'modern', we seem to have decided to focus a lot more on our 'rights'. We want to live our lives as we want them regardless of how evil or ridiculous our choices become. Each person wants to be minister, teacher, president and counsellor and everything else for their own lives. So we question everything and everyone who tries to give us an instruction that seems to infringe on those rights. Children no longer respond to adults' bidding by doing as they are told but instead respond by asking why they should do what the adult says. There seems to be an intense tug-a-war in most interactions with everyone expressing their opinion and challenging authority. Our mouths have run way ahead of both our ears and common sense. Looking around our communities we can see the results of our disobedience, the lifestyles, the choices, the habits, the rebellion, the general nastiness that is no longer challenged as it would have been in the past.

The widow of Zarephath (1 Kings 17) and the prophet's widow (2 Kings 4) both provide excellent examples of people who soaked their lives in obedience. Both were in dire straits, in a life or death situation and when they were faced with a solution for their problems it was a ridiculous one according to the standards of this world. But they soaked it all in obedience, receiving instructions that made no sense but which because they obeyed, provided a way out of their season of serious lack.

The widow at Zarephath was desperate. She had a young child to feed just one more time before they both died. They were virtually on their last meal. Elijah appeared and this woman must have been relieved to see him thinking that the man of God was there to pray for her and offer a 'practical' solution to her hopeless situation. Instead he asked her to go ahead and prepare her last meal and feed him before she even fed her son. I can just imagine what people would be saying if this happened today. By the end of the day the whole scenario would have gone viral; there would be utter outrage at this man of God who would take food from a baby's mouth as it were. Various professionals would be alerted and investigations would speedily get underway. This man of God would be in big trouble and probably have his face plastered all over the television networks.

But this woman though reluctant knew that she really didn't have anything to lose. If it meant they would die a day earlier than expected they were still doomed to die or so she thought. So she fed the man of God, she obeyed his request and in the end she benefited more than she could have ever dreamed. She got her exceedingly abundantly above anything she could think or ask (Ephesians 3:20). God rewarded her obedience so much that she never had to worry about feeding her son again.

The prophet's widow on the other hand was told to go and gather containers. Empty containers! She could easily have left the man of God and gone to look for people who could lend her money or help her in a more 'realistic' way. What good are containers, and empty ones at that to a hungry woman and her children? But she obeyed the servant of God and she never lacked and her children were not taken away from her to pay their father's debt. She was told to pour oil into many containers, the little bit of oil that she had could not fill one container, but it became the seed that was then multiplied to fill all the empty jars she had gathered. She demonstrated a double-pronged obedience, she was told to gather containers and to make sure she gathered not 'just a few' (2 Kings 4:3) and that is what she did.

I think obedience is difficult sometimes because it means we are setting our own desires, our will and our pride aside. Disobedience is a battle of wills with the person that is expected to obey refusing to acknowledge and bow to someone else's directive. Disobedience can be revealed in the form of rebellion, of doing what goes against expectations or instruction. Obedience also means trusting without knowing the end result. It's putting your life in someone else's hands and many of us struggle with that.

Consider 1 Samuel 1:23 and how strongly the prophet Samuel spoke against disobedience or rebellion likening it to the sin of divination or witchcraft:

For rebellion is like the sin of divination, and arrogance like the evil of idolatry. Because you have rejected the word of The Lord, he has rejected you as king

It's difficult to deal with a disobedient child or as a teacher to have a child in your class who never seems to do what they are told. Their disobedience can set a bad example for other children or it can disrupt lessons. Sometimes this disobedience can have dire consequences, can lead to endangering of life and can lead to privileges being withdrawn or withheld. A disobedient student makes it hard for you to teach the class and they demand attention unduly to themselves at the expense of the whole class. We understand this on a human level. Even the worst parents who have never invested anything in their children's lives still expect to be obeyed. But we seem to find it difficult to see the parallels between our human relationships and our relationship with our Father God. We demand obedience but we don't give it when it is expected of us. We seem to think that it is okay to expect to reap obedience even though we have never sowed it in anyone's life. We are upset when our children are disobedient but we forget that we are also children and that our father expects from us what we are expecting to get from our children.

But in the same way disobedience has consequences, obedience also does. There are benefits that are tied to our obedience, blessings that come our way because we have been obedient:

If you are willing and obedient, you will eat the best from the land (Isaiah 1:19).

There are many more illustrations of lives soaked both in obedience and disobedience in the Word of God; lives whose positive or negative lessons can help us understand obedience a bit more. Some people obeyed without question, others like Jonah obeyed after going through some trauma, and yet others like Samson suffered heavy losses for their disobedience. What a lot of disaster we could avoid if we learned from those that have gone before us. How much easier could life be for young people if they listened to and obeyed their parents? Heart-ache could be averted; dismal mistakes could be avoided if people listened to each other and honoured the structures that are put in place to create functional relationships.

Maybe the best lessons on obedience come from our spiritual brothers and sisters, the Israelites. God had a plan for them and he sent Moses to execute that plan, which was to lead the Israelites from slavery to a place where they owned the land they were led to. God's plans for them were good, but before they could reach Canaan, in order for them to get to Canaan, the Israelites had to follow Moses, they had to obey what God said through Moses and unfortunately they didn't obey and they paid a very high price for their disobedience, a short journey became a long forty year trip (Deuteronomy 1:2). Also because of their disobedience, many died in the wilderness (Hebrews 3:17-19). Unfortunately also those who disobeyed were not allowed to get to the Promised Land (Hebrews 3:19). Each time they disobeyed God they paid a hefty price, each time they obeyed they also reaped the benefits. Similar experiences are reflected in our own lives when we disobey biblical principles and end up in debt, in bad relationships, missing out on opportunities, hooking up with bad friends and so on.

God seems to value our obedience in part because it is an expression of our trust in him. It shows that we trust that his plans for us really are plans for good and not for evil and that his divine intention is to give us a hope and a future (Jeremiah 29:11). Because he is a God of order (1 Corinthians 14:33) there is the expectation that we will obey not only him but his word and also his servants (2 Chronicles 20:20) and the people he has placed in authority over us.

Soaking our lives in obedience is a choice. Disobedience is also a choice. We are always given the option to choose one path or the other. We are speaking spirits that have the power to decide and in so doing we determine our own fate in so many ways as angels respond to our words as they did when Daniel prayed (Daniel 10:12):

Then he continued, "Do not be afraid, Daniel. Since the first day that you set your mind to gain understanding and to humble yourself before your God, your words were heard, and I have come in response to them.

11

Joshua soaked it in battle

SOAK IT!

Reading through the book of Joshua we encounter a warrior not many people did or can match. His whole recorded life after Moses died was a life of war. We are not told much about him other than that he was the son of Nun, and that he was Moses' aide (Exodus 24: 13) and right-hand man (Numbers 11:28) but his battles are chronicled for posterity. We know him as a man who won just about every battle he went into.

Joshua knew that he was supposed to lead the Israelites into the Promised Land. He knew also that the land wouldn't come to them! They had to go and take it and possess it. So he went to war to take what he knew was his. What a difference there would be in our finances, spiritual life, relationships and all facets of life if we did a Joshua on the issues that assail us, if we went out to get what is ours rather than wait for things to happen or to come to us. How many children would be better off if parents fought for them, how many marriages would defy divorce if both partners fought for their marriage rather than fight each other? We have to fight for the things we have been promised, for the things we know are ours to possess.

A lot of the time we don't get anything because we wait for things to fall into our laps. We have varying degrees of spiritual laziness and a spiritual spoilt brat syndrome as well in that we want God to prepare the food, bring it to us, put a bib over our clothes and encourage us to open our mouths and eat! We know the food is there because God has told us about it and our spiritual noses twitch each time we hear the Word and know that something good is cooking. But we just can't seem to get up and go get it. Then we become filled with envy and jealousy when some people refuse to sit and starve and choose instead to go and get what God has dished up. God has promised us a lot of things in his word and his promises are sure:

God's way is perfect. All The Lord's promises prove true. He is a shield for all who look to him for protection (Psalm 18:30 NLT)

For no matter how many promises God has made, they are "Yes" in Christ. And so through him the "Amen" is spoken by us to the glory of God (2 Corinthians 1:20)

Not one of all The Lord's good promises to Israel failed; every one was fulfilled (Joshua 21:45)

We can't keep 'waiting on The Lord' for promises already written and spelt out for us. Joshua went to battle, so should we. He engaged in battles to possess, so should we. If we read about Joshua we will find a pattern or formula that is as relevant and applicable today as it was in his day. We too can possess physical land, emotional, spiritual, relational, familial, marital and every other land that has already been assigned to us by our loving father who has apportioned an inheritance for us.

JOSHUA KNEW THE LAND

He was leading his people into a land that he already knew because he went to spy it first. He didn't just chance on the land. He took time to familiarise himself with his promise and to count the cost (Luke 14:28).

Looking back over my life I think this has been one of the weakest aspects of my journey to get what God has assigned to me. I sort of happened on things, stumbled into them. I didn't realise how important it was to see the land first so that I could understand what was in it, what strategies I needed to employ to win it and how to prepare for possession. I got to places purely by grace because God loved me enough to preserve and to persevere with me. I did not have the wisdom or the courage to sit and plan. In fact the biggest problem was that I didn't even know that God's plans for me really were plans for good and not evil (Jeremiah 29:11). For some reason I believed in qualifying for things, qualifying for love, qualifying for blessings. I didn't really have the heart knowledge that Christ was not angry with me and that regardless of the mess that had been my life he actually loved me and I really was and am his beloved and precious to him:

Since you are precious and honored in my sight, and because I love you, I will give people in exchange for you, nations in exchange for your life (Isaiah 43:4)

I had a head knowledge of scripture, a very academic kind of knowledge. I could quote the scripture but I didn't really believe that it applied to me. I could even preach and teach the scripture and write about it and help people who needed help, but it was always for others. I had already agreed with myself that I was disqualified. People had seen to it that I knew that I was disqualified; I didn't fit into the blessed crowd. So I accepted that and believed that my portion was the crumbs that everyone else dropped as they sat at table, I believed that my portion was the second-hand clothes no one else wanted anymore and I became a beggar in my own father's house.

But this is where the awesomeness of God really hits me. I am so grateful that as I have continued refusing to neglect the coming together of the saints, he has not neglected to continue equipping me, opening my eyes, redirecting my attention to what he has already done. He has faithfully kept talking to me again about my worth and my inheritance, my rights as his beloved daughter, as someone who has been washed, totally cleaned and washed by the blood of The Lamb. So finally, after a long run with my eyes on the ground, God has done a Psalm 3:3 in me and I now walk with my head held high. I have my moments when I forget, when I am overwhelmed by good things happening to me and I start having that sense of unworthiness. But Jehovah, the Creator of all that was created loves me and he has seen to it that the cave is no longer my place of residence. He has restored not only my soul as mentioned in Psalm 23 but my very life. I am in awe of such a God.

So now I know that I need to look ahead and see what God has already promised me and direct my faith and my focus towards that. You can't buy furniture for a house you haven't seen or at least seen detailed photos and plans for. You need to know the room sizes so that you don't buy furniture that is too big or small or furniture that can't fill in spaces adequately. The viewing is crucial for the dream to be a reality, transferred from something in the realm of imagination to something in the zone of reality, tangibility and possibility. The Word has to become flesh (John 1:14), it has to be translated from something I read, hear, believe and speak to something I live in, drive, eat, give and celebrate.

It's not surprising that drunkards tend to breed drunkards, graduates, graduates and people on welfare also tend to perpetuate the trend generationally. Of course this is sort of a blanket statement and there are always people who defy the expected, but I am sure there are sufficient numbers and statistics to verify the above statement. A child whose parents are illiterate may not go far with their education as there is no parental or familial precedence or role model. Tradition tends to repeat itself and the apple does tend to fall quite near the tree.

Children who come from households and families where work

is shunned see that as the way to go, that is the environment that nurtures them and that is the reality they know. Thank God for his grace which changes lives so that all things become new (Revelation 21:5; 2 Corinthians 5:17). By his word he can change a person and separate those things that have become the accepted norm for them:

For the word of God is quick, and powerful, and sharper than any two-edged sword, piercing even to the dividing asunder of soul and spirit, and of the joints and marrow, and is a discerner of the thoughts and intents of the heart. (Hebrews 4:12 KJV)

It is important to present the mind with different possibilities from what we know or were raised around. God grants the desires of our hearts (Psalm 37:4) but for many of us, there is a need to change these desires, to enlarge what we visualise for ourselves and our families. It is free to look, to get into a good hotel and have a look around, or to view a house, or test-drive a particular car. It's free to seek godly connections that have succeeded in what you are as yet attempting to make your reality. I'd rather God grants my desires now than 10 years ago. Ten years ago my desires were small, selfish, without clarity and superficial. I have now allowed the place of the habitation of my dreams to be enlarged (Isaiah 54:2) so that I now also know that as God grants the desires of my heart now they will not only have huge results but also huge impact not just on my life but on people around me. Like Joshua I have been visiting and spying my promised land, in fact I'm still in there, I haven't finished surveying the place and pegging it yet but I have started.

JOSHUA INQUIRED Of THE LORD.

Before he went to war Joshua checked in with The Lord. I believe that the main reason why Joshua succeeded was because he didn't try to do battle without divine help. Here was a warrior who knew the extent of both his strength and weakness. He had no illusions about what he could do and where his victory came from so he always consulted with the source of his help just like we should look unto Jesus, the author and perfecter of our faith (Hebrews 12:2) just like we should look to the hills from where our help comes (Psalm 121).

If we are truly and honestly reflective, we can admit that a lot of our failure has come as a result our own manipulative tendencies. We have not sought the wisdom and counsel of the omniscient, omnipresent and omnipotent God who is our shepherd if we allow him to be (Psalm 23).

JOSHUA INVOLVED ALL THE TRIBES

Joshua was not selfish in his quest to possess the land. He involved all the tribes in the acquisition of land for each other.

We recently had a celebration about five months after my mum went home. It occurred at a time when none of my siblings and I had cash to spare and it could easily have been a real flop. But as I looked back over it at the end of the day I could not ignore the faithfulness of God. One of the reasons why we managed to do the memorial and feed about 200 people was because a handful of us chipped in whatever little we had, I believe God then stretched the rest so that in the end we even took some food home and that fed family members who stayed with us for some time after the celebration service.

One person may have the desire to achieve a task but what they have may not stretch far enough to make a difference, but when a few people pool their resources together, where one could only make a tiny dent they can make major inroads into solving a problem. The bible illustrates this beautifully as it demonstrates synergy in Deuteronomy 32:30 and Matthew 18:19.

Joshua was obviously a wise leader who recognised this fact

and he made sure that even those tribes who had already got their inheritance still joined in the battle to ensure that every child of God ended up in their place of inheritance. Think about the difference we could make in each other's lives if we pooled our resources to help each other.

JOSHUA WENT TO WAR

This is a lesson most people still need to learn. Things don't just show up, they don't walk into our homes, wardrobes, garages and bank accounts. There is a certain level of warring that is required for us to get anything we need. The great thing about our warring as children of God is the fact that we don't do it alone. God is with us, he fights alongside us, he does not leave us to face the enemy on our own. He tells us that he will neither leave nor forsake us (Deuteronomy 31:6). I love how he shows off and is in the thick of battles, ensuring and guaranteeing our victory, but we have to get up off our backsides and go to war. Here is an excellent illustration of how our divine partner works:

And as they were fleeing from Israel, they were on the slope of Beth-horon, and Yahweh threw huge stones from the heaven on them as far as Azekah; and more died by the hail stones than those whom the Israelites killed by the sword (Joshua 10:11 LEB).

We may no longer have to acquire weapons in the natural to go and fight a human enemy who inhabits land that is ours but we have possessions that need to be fought for spiritually and in the engagement of our hands or our minds as weapons of war. God still teaches our hands to war and our fingers to do battle or to fight against whatever enemies are attacking us (Psalm 18:1). He still expects us to fight and to win.

We all know people whose hands are always stretched out to receive. It never occurs to them that as they stretch out their hands, they could put something in it to bless someone else. It's all about them. They have not learned as yet that if they want things they should work, they should war against the poverty they are surrounded by. It's interesting that the bible says that a person who does not work must not eat (2 Thessalonians 3:10). There appears to be an expectation of reciprocity, as one works one receives and can eat from the fruit of their own labour.

God also promises to bless not the outstretched hand but the fruit of our hands (Psalm 128:2). He rewards what we do, our labour, our work, our stepping out in faith to do something be it ploughing and sowing a field, or buying and selling small or big things, be it going to work for someone else or setting up our own business through which we also become employers.

143

Whatever effort we make he is not unjust to forget it, to ignore the labour of our love (Hebrews 6:10).

Whatever issues and situations may be invading your personal space need to be dealt with and it's not always other people that should deal with them. We each have both accountability and responsibility over what happens in our lives, the time to point fingers and blame has to come to an end at some point. We have been given stewardship over our lives and we will need to and have to give an account of what we did to secure our inheritance. The begging spirit and the selfish, always-looking-inward spirit both need banishment if we are indeed to taste and see that The Lord is good as he comes alongside us to help us acquire what he has always said belongs to us (Psalm 34:8).

Fathers need to show their sons and daughters that there is no shame in working and providing for their families, in fact there is honour. The bible castigates men who do not provide for their families and compares them to the 'infidel' :

But if any provide not for his own, and specially for those of his own house, he hath denied the faith, and is worse than an infidel (KJV).

Spongers rear spongers, but people with healthy work ethics will hopefully pass this on to their children. Mothers who are lazy nurture in their children a dependent spirit. They focus on nailing a rich man at all costs because they have never been taught that they can generate wealth and don't need to trick anyone out of their hard-earned income. Needy people are not pleasant to have around, they multiply your outgoings and they usually see this as their right rather than as your generosity.

Poverty and lack are horrible enemies which do not depart through charity. It is true that it is better to teach a man to fish than to give him a fish. Once he has fed off the one fish you gave him he will be back for more again and again until he becomes a pest. Instead if a person is taught life-skills, they can look after themselves and their family. This all sounds so easy and simple but there are people who dole out things to people and thrive on the dependency created, but this is not to the benefit of the recipient of the charity. People have two feet (unless of course they have had an accident of some sort) so they should be allowed to stand on those two feet, any crutch they are offered becomes a hindrance to normalcy.

Proverbs 31:10-31 highlights how a wise woman goes to war against every conceivable enemy that can fight against her and her family. She does not sit back and expect her marriage, workers, children, character and finances to work themselves out. She engages in spiritual, financial and all other battles to assure and ensure the well-being of her family. Like Joshua she goes to war.

Food does not walk onto our dining tables. It has to be sourced from somewhere. Clothes don't grow on our backs. They also need to be sourced from somewhere. In all labour there is profit (Proverbs 14:23), there is food, clothing, shelter, holidays, family provision and everything else we need. We have to go to war through jobs, businesses, projects and everything else we can put our hands to for God to bless.

JOSHUA WON HIS BATTLES

This makes me think of the difference between a flaccid and a turgid plant stem. Both are stems and both have the same potential to bear fruit. Looking at them, one sees contrasts of strength and weakness, despair and resilience.

A flaccid stem has given up the battle. It has wilted under the strain of heat or draught. Rather than standing up tall and rigid it is bent over and drooping. It has not heard of Psalm 3:3:

But thou, O LORD, art a shield for me; my glory, and the lifter up of mine head (KJV)

So in the onslaught of trouble it has no staying power. Its spirit cannot sustain it (Proverbs 18:14), it has not built up stamina and endurance and so it hangs its head in shame as if there is no hope for it. Its inner condition is reflected into its physical, its hopelessness is displayed in negative talk, its dryness showing through ineffectiveness and lack of impact. What is inside is manifested outside. It is a flaccid plant and there are flaccid people who have not taken time to stoke up strength for the day of trouble and testing, they have not hidden a reserve of the active word (Hebrews 4:12) in their hearts, so when challenges come they have nothing inside to help them fight what is on the outside.

Joshua shows evidence of turgidity. He went to war to win and he didn't allow heat or rain, trouble or drought to hinder his victory. When time stood in his way to accomplish what he needed to do he commanded it to stand still (Joshua 10:13). He didn't just fight in the natural; he knew that his success would not be by might nor by his own power but by

God's spirit, by the supernatural intervention of God (Zechariah 4:6). So he defied natural laws and relied on his position in the kingdom to make every system work on his behalf.

Joshua won his battles. He didn't quit and neither should we. We cannot afford to shy away from battles more so since our victory is already assured. God already told us that the battle is not ours, it belongs to him (1 Samuel 17:47; 2 Chronicles 20:15), we just need to show up and do our part knowing also that we can do all things through Christ who gives us strength (Philippians 4:13).

The enemy does not put up a half- hearted defense around the things God has given us so we cannot afford to put up a lackluster challenge, but have to go out all guns blazing to possess our land. Limpid and flaccid spirits can't win our inheritance for us but persistence, determination and sheer bull-headedness is what will make us win. We can't afford to give up and turn back when things get tough. We have to keep at it. There can only be one winner in respect to our inheritance, it can't be a win-win symbiotic situation, there is only one winner and that has to be us.

Our victory also has to be total. We cannot afford to leave

some previous tenants in our land, we have to drive out each squatter group and take full possession of what is ours, of what our father has signed over to us as our inheritance.

12

Nathaniel soaked it in soundness of character

SOAK IT!

In John 1:47 Nathaniel was referred to by The Lord himself as a man in whom there is no guile or deceit. We all love compliments and to be appreciated and acknowledged when we do things right. But the people around us don't know us well enough to unequivocally vouch for the soundness of our character. This is why there is such shock when a loved one is arrested, such horror when affairs are discovered, such grief when the true financial state of a family is revealed. We don't really know anyone, even those supposedly closest to us.

But for Christ, the King of kings, The Lord of lords, the son of the Most High God, the integral part of creation to say that there is no guile in someone that means there really is no guile. There is nothing hidden before The Lord (Hebrews 4:13; Luke 8:17), he is omnipotent, omniscient and omnipresent. As a result there is no higher compliment than that which comes from an all-seeing omniscient God. This was a man in whom there really was no deceit.

What a blessing for people to know you and know that what they see is indeed what they get. How precious for a spouse or loved one to know also that they can trust you implicitly, that there will never be any nasty relational, financial or other surprises. What a joy it must be to know that when your spouse says that they are at work they really are at work and they are actually working. What a comfort to know that when your children call you and tell you that they are staying behind to finish some work at school or college that is what they are actually doing. In these days of mobile technology a person could be anywhere when they say they are in another place. What a privilege to be a parent to or married to or in any way connected to a Nathaniel in whom there really is no deceit.

Unfortunately secrecy reigns in a lot of relationships even those among believers. Multiple phones are bought and hidden away, bank statements are secreted in drawers and safes and lies spew out of the same mouths that praise and supposedly worship God on a Sunday. Thank God there are Nathaniels, genuine and sincere men and women who ensure that their 'yea' is indeed 'yea' and their 'nay' remains 'nay' (James 5:12; Matthew 5:37). It is great to be someone your circle can trust and vouch for without fear or concern.

Jonathan is another wonderful example of someone who

soaks it all in sound character. He was a genuine friend. He was a friend to the point where he forfeited his own claim to the throne because he was an honourable man (1 Samuel 20), someone who honoured God's choice. He stood for what was right even though it meant that he went against his father and endorsed David for the throne. Jonathan's friendship was sincere and his love was demonstrative and genuine. Having just a couple of such people in your circle would be awesome. You would know they have got your back and that when they make a promise you can take their word for it.

I recall a situation some years ago where these two ladies I knew were very close friends. They did everything together. One of them started dating this guy but that didn't alter the friendship between the two women. They carried on. In the end, the man ended up with the other friend. She took her best friend's man. I'm sure her friend trusted her, but that trust was misplaced and in the end she was stabbed in the back by the very person she trusted. There was guile in this friend, the other lady didn't know and so she trusted two people she never should have. In the end she realised that her trust had been misplaced. She realised that the people she thought were her friends should never have been allowed near her.

Elisha is another excellent example of men and women who are loyal, not like Reuben whose own father described him as being 'unstable like water' (Genesis 49:4). When your own parent describes you that way then you know for a fact you have issues. Reuben's character was analysed by his own father and he was found to be shifting, unstable, not solid, changing and fluctuating between opinions. You couldn't trust him because you never really knew where he stood on any issue; he shifted around, fluid like water. He changed from solid to liquid and when necessary possibly for self-preservation to a gaseous state. He couldn't be trusted or relied on. Shifty and unstable people make the worst friends. You can sit with them and plan something today only to find out they have left you in a lurch; they have made other decisions behind your back.

But Elisha was to Elijah what Joshua must have been to Moses. He was loyal to the end, reliable, dependable, there when needed, there as a successor who had been trained on the job. He wasn't like some of the interlopers who hang around wanting to step into someone's shoes without ever having gone through the appropriate life experiences, without counting the cost. They see the final product and want it, desire it, covert it. They see the outward results and want to have it all without ever finding out how the person they covet got to where they are. They don't give their spirit time to grow strong, time to build up stamina. They see it and they want it. They want to be Pastors over thousands of people yet they have never sowed the seed of discipleship or sonship. They don't realise that there is preparation time, there is training time, there is growing up time and there is qualification and testing time before things can be entrusted to us. Elisha like Joshua soaked it all in soundness of character, in being a man others could rely on. He didn't hurry to become the leader but took time to learn and follow Elijah until his own time came.

Marriages would last if they were between Elisha and Joshua-like characters; people who are in it to win it, in it for the long haul. Companies wouldn't cheat people of life savings if they were led by people of sound character. Nations would thrive if their leaders were not in it for what they could get out of it and only for themselves. If leaders cared about the people they led, if they were faithful stewards of the people and resources God put in their hands then nations would thrive. But unfortunately, there aren't many that Christ could look at among the entire aggregate of global leaders, and say that they are leaders without guile. There aren't many that he would recommend as great leaders or many that have the interest of the people they lead at heart.

Another wonderful example of a man of integrity was Aaron. He had his moments like we all do. He rebelled against his leader (Numbers 12), he pandered to the demands of a spoilt bunch of ungrateful people whose Father did everything for them yet they still ended up erecting an idol (Exodus 32). But despite all his shortcomings, he is a man that stood with Moses and lifted his arms, supported him for the common good of victory for the Israelites (Exodus 17:12). Aaron served his younger brother. He submitted to another man's vision and stood by him through some very trying times. He too was a man of sound character. He didn't allow his age to make him act superior to his younger brother. Instead he recognised God's calling on Moses and stood by him.

I think from Aaron we also learn similar lessons we get from Jonathan. We don't judge people by their age or their station in life. Instead as believers we must pray for eyes to see what God sees. We have to pray for anointing sensitivity so that we stop knowing, judging and relating to people after the flesh (2 Corinthians 5:16) and start seeing them and relating with them according to what God has put in them. I applaud parents who can sit in a church and be preached to by their sons and daughters. They are people of sound character. They are also so confident in themselves and their self-worth that they don't try to use their parental positions in places where they shouldn't count. They honor who God honors and bless who God blesses. In the end they receive both honor and blessings themselves. Their seed of humility is accepted and multiplied by the man who stills the water (Mark 4:39), as they humble themselves, it is not just to people but to The Lord who called them so they get lifted up (James 4:10; 1 Peter 5:6). It is a proud spirit that thinks it should always be the one that knows best.

There are many other examples of people of sound character in the bible, men and women who could be called upon to serve without expecting anything in return. Uriah was a good example. He refused to enjoy home comforts when his peers were at war (2 Samuel 11). He could have gone home and had a hot meal, spent quality time with his wife and taken advantage of the time off the battle. But Uriah couldn't enjoy these things knowing that his friends were fighting. He was a man of honour. His character made it difficult for David to pull a fast one over him.

There are some people who open their mouths and they have become so proficient at fibbing that you can never differentiate between their lies and their truth. Nothing within them warns them anymore, their conscience is so seared that lying comes as easily as truth. 1 Timothy 4:2 in NLT is quite blunt:

These people are hypocrites and liars, and their consciences are dead.

A person whose life is soaked in soundness of character, a person in whom there is no guile is one that can be trusted, whose word means something and whose promises are sincere. They do what they say they will do. Their promise is a covenant which cannot be broken or altered, just like our father's covenant with us (Psalm 89:34). There are people who no longer realise that they are lying. They are always promising to do things; they are quick to make pledges. They don't realise that making promises and not keeping them is just as bad as lying, in fact it is lying. It is better to keep quiet or to wait until you know for sure that you can do what you say, otherwise you become a recipient of rolled eyes whenever you open your mouth.

I remember a time my dad was assigned to his first diplomatic post in a European country. He did all he could to find accommodation but for some reason he couldn't. At one time he was offered a house that shared a fence with the local dumpsite which for obvious reasons he refused to accept.

They stayed in a hotel for quite a while which was difficult for them as they couldn't settle and get on with the job they had come to do. Later on my dad found out that he wasn't being allocated a house because the people expected a bribe from him. Needless to say they never did get the bribe, he called his bosses who then dealt with the issue in such a way that apologies were sent and more than one house made available for them to choose from. He refused to lower his standards. Even at work my dad soaked his dealings with people in honesty and truth and refused to dabble in 'acceptable' practices of bribery and deceit.

I suppose in all humanity is a tendency to veer towards self-preservation even sometimes at the expense of truth. But it is crucial to look within ourselves and see what sort of people we have become. Has life and its issues so hardened us that we no longer know basic right from wrong? Have we become so focused on the self that we no longer care about who we are in the lives of the people around us? A person of sound character can be trusted even in situations where he does not gain anything. He will deal fairly with people, he will not use the unfair balances (dishonest scales, false scales, deceitful scales, balance of deceit) referred to in Proverbs 20:23.

The great thing is that it is never too late for any of us to change if we want to. So maybe it's time to ask for God's help in transforming our characters so that we can soak our lives and relationships in soundness of character.

13

The Mary's and certain women **soaked it in the presence of The Lord**

SOAK IT!

The women in the New Testament got it right. They were an interesting mix of named and unnamed women. They were an aggregate of checkered pasts, miraculous births, dubious character, wealth and influence, healed and delivered, wives, single ladies and more. But they had one thing in common; they saw The Lord and realised that he was more than just a teacher or prophet. They realised that he was worth their time, their commitment and even their substance. They realised also that it was important for them to spend time with him, to minister to his needs and those of his ministry and to be taught at his feet. They soaked their lives in his presence daily finding ways they could be a blessing to him and to those around him.

It's interesting how many people in the bible are not mentioned by name and yet their deeds, their faith, their service are all recorded. It is almost as if The Lord does not want to detract from the revelation we should get from their lives by cluttering our minds with mindless superficial detail. These people are as much a part of our cloud of witnesses (Hebrew 12:1) as the well-known and name Sarahs, and Davids, the Deborah's and the Caleb's.

Our focus is not supposed to be on their identity, the way we would define them by their family name, gender, nationality, ethnicity or whatever other categories we may want to box them into. A sifting has already been done for us and the superficial has been dispensed with so that we see what God sees and what he wants us to see as well. So there is as much to learn from the woman with the issue of blood as there is from Mary. There is significance in the lessons we learn from the widow offering her 2 mites (Luke 21:1-4) as there is from Abraham and Hannah offering their sons to The Lord (Genesis 22; 1 Samuel 2). We learn as much from the man at the gate to the temple called Beautiful (Acts 3:2) as we do from Peter's unnamed mother-in-law (Matthew 18:14) or from Sheerah the female architect (1 Chronicles 7:24).

It's not the external things that matter, it's not even the rank, or the position, the job or the career, the family one comes from or whose wife or husband they are. What counts is what is within a person and our lives would be so much richer if we stopped focusing on people's country of origin, or their age, skin colour or socio-economic status and look instead at the heart.

As we look through the Word of God we realise our error in elevating people beyond where we should place them, turning them into idols. Even as Christians it is so easy to idolise people and apportion them a level of significance they do not deserve. We can be as guilty as the world of putting people on pedestals and according them a place we should only accord to God. An idol does not have to be an object or an ugly statue; it can be just as much a person as it can be a thing. It's the awe we accord it, and the adulation we think it deserves that elevates it to idol status.

The bible exhorts us to look to the hills where our help comes from (Psalm 121) and to look unto Jesus the author and perfecter of our faith (Hebrews 12:2). It tells us also about the name that is above every name (Philippians 2:9) the only name worth name-dropping about. Had God wanted us to focus on nomenclature he would have directed our attention to names but instead he teaches us crucial lessons using unnamed people. He seems to underplay the person and boost up the worker of the miracles that person receives. When we look at the lives of so many unnamed people in the Word, they didn't try to push through to places of recognition, they did what they did without fanfare and even though people may not have known them, Christ did.

Think about the woman with the issue of blood. She tried to get close to Jesus without making an announcement of her intentions. She didn't tell everybody how much she bombarded the gates of heaven till she got her healing. She was prepared to touch The Lord and step away but he brought attention to her, her miracle, her faith and her healing. She soaked herself in the healing present in his presence and he rewarded her faith by adding her to the annals of faith which have been accessed by millions over the centuries.

There is a group of women referred to only as 'certain women' (Luke 8:2) who followed The Lord and ministered to him. A few of their group are named and God has a reason for the detail he gives about some and the lack of it for others. Joanna the wife of Chuza is mentioned by name as are Susanna and Mary Magdalene. These women spent time with The Lord; they soaked their lives in his presence. He became a focus of their lives, their ministry and their substance. His vision became their vision and they are recorded for our sake. Those in their group who are not mentioned by name are mentioned all the same, their actions are recorded; their faith and faithfulness are also recorded.

Regardless of whether we are named well-known people or apparently insignificant unnamed people, we can impact the church, and the world around us. Our positions, names, qualifications or lack of should have no bearing on what we can accomplish as ministers in God's house or as people who are blessed to be a blessing. We can soak our lives in his presence and receive mercy and find grace to help us in our time of need (Hebrews 4:16).

The enemy wants us to focus on the negatives, on what we don't have, on what we cannot be. If we continue to look at our circumstances we can't look at Christ. If we can't look at him he cannot communicate with us as the author and perfector of our faith (Hebrews 12:2). He loves us and already did what needed to be done when he said 'It is finished' (John 19:30). He wants to relate with us as he teaches us who we are in him. But if we soak our lives in pity parties, in feeling sorry for ourselves, in feeling inferior to everyone around us then we have no room to receive the gift of grace extended to us. We have no time to praise him and welcome him into our circumstances. His word tells us that he dwells in the praises, not the grumblings and rumblings of his people (Psalm 22:3). If we want to soak our lives in his presence then our language has to change from complaining to worshipping, from self-pity to confidence.

We have to praise him till we can grasp the truth in the fact that he bore our pain already (Isaiah 53), as he is so are we (1 John 4:17), and that we are heirs together with Christ (Romans 8:17). We are not taking a test to see if we qualify for the things he has bought for us. It is not about us, we already are the righteousness of God in Christ (2 Corinthians 5:21) our own efforts at righteousness are regarded as filthy rags (Isaiah 64:6). As we soak in his presence, as we lift him up, we become part of his force of attraction, drawing people to him, to his love and goodness (John 12:32). We have a part to play in making our God attractive to the people around us. They can't see him physically but they see us, the heirs together with Christ (Romans 8:17)

When we as believers vie for positions, when we compete for a place of recognition we shift our eyes and the eyes of people looking at us and learning from us. When leaders fight other leaders and publicly discredit those of the body of Christ who stumble and fall, they block people's sight from seeing Christ to seeing what these irresponsible leaders are focusing on. Sometimes people don't realise that we are all part of the same body and each branch should focus on what it is supposed to supply (Ephesians 4:16). But instead, so many times each branch is trying to outshine the other, legs are trying to act like eyes and arms are trying to be spleens. We end up showing the world a very weird-looking church because we are not soaking our life in Christ but soaking it in self- importance instead. We sometimes forget that people are only drawn to Christ if we lift him up (John 12:32).

Leaders need to show people Christ not gimmicks and tricks. When hurting people come to church, they don't need anyone telling them off for their mistakes, they already know they have messed up which is why they come in the first place. If our eyes are focused on Christ, if we are soaked in him, people who come alongside us have to also come in contact with the Lamb that was slain for them and they then receive help and healing.

A life soaked in Christ's presence will exude Christ. It will attract people to Christ. And we know that when people are drawn to Christ, when they encounter the Prince of Peace, The Lord of lords, the King of kings, their lives will never be the same. They will encounter the virtue that flows from him, salvation, healing, peace, comfort, help, transformation and all the good things that are in him.

14

God soaks it in order

SOAK IT!

Sometimes things don't work out in our lives because everything is so chaotic! We don't know what we are doing from day to day, life just happens, we just stumble into things, reacting to the various crisis as they emerge. But God is a God of order (1 Corinthians 14:33, Genesis 1). He doesn't just stumble onto things; he is a God of order.

If God didn't care about the state of our affairs, why would he promise us that he would perfect that which concerns us (Psalm 138:8)? Why would he be concerned about ensuring that all things work together for our good (Romans 8:28)? He is the God of order; he created an orderly world and bequeathed to us an orderly inheritance which though complex is orderly. Or at least it was until we abused it.

I look at my life and I know that the times I have made good progress in whatever area has been when I took time to sit down and draw up some kind of plan so that ahead of time I

167

knew what I needed to accomplish in a day or a week. My calendar has been a crucial tool to keep me focused. This has been particularly important since I became self-employed. It is amazing how easy it is to drift from day to day without achieving or accomplishing anything at all. Picture this very real scenario:

You wake up and eat then watch a program or two on the television, before checking emails and Facebook posts. After this you are hungry again and thirsty and you return to the kitchen for a snack then decide that you want to bake because you haven't had a cake for a while and your sweet tooth is clamoring for attention. You yield to the sugar craving and bake. By the time you finish you sit down to catch up with friends on the phone. You decide to have a taste of the cake, so you make a cuppa to go with it. You sit down intending to watch a short program as you eat but there is this film you have been intending to watch for a while so you decide to just watch a small part of it. By the time the film ends you take the dishes to the kitchen and decide to wash up. Your phone rings just as you finish this and you talk to your friend for 30 minutes. Your eyes stray to the clock on the wall and you are shocked to find out that it is already 3.30pm and you need to start dinner.

The day wasn't planned for so whatever demanded attention was given the attention. Nothing is accomplished and this day can be perpetuated with nothing accomplished by the end of the week, the month, the year, the life.

The bible tells us that as Christ is so are we in this world (1 John 4:17). This being the case, if he is the God of order then so should we be. We have to consciously create some order out of the chaos in our lives. Planning and sticking to those plans and goals is crucial to our achieving the things we know we should achieve. They don't happen by themselves. Our lives have to be soaked in the God of order so that we can learn from him.

Genesis 8:22 talks about a pattern set in place by God which applies to us now and has been applicable in all the generations before us: seed time and harvest time. Things don't happen at random, we don't reap as a result of a big bang theory but as a result of what we sow. There is order to our lives initiated by our adhering to 'how things are done'. If we give we receive (Luke 6:38), if we withhold then we also minimise what we can get back (Proverbs 11:24). God does not leave our futures to chance; he has put things in place, guidance that can help us achieve the destiny he has in store for us.

169

Mark 4:28 presents another scenario showing God's order:

For the earth bringeth forth fruit of herself; first the blade, then the ear, after that the full corn in the ear (KJV).

Human beings can be so fickle. We want certain results and demand them but we don't want to do whatever it is that can yield said results. We want a wonderful marriage but we don't want to put in the work needed to make it so. We want a six-figure salary even though we never tried to get a qualification that can at least authenticate our seriousness about the job market. We forget that there are certain laws that are God-made which we have to live by. We can't eat chips, cake, burgers, bacon and everything else we want daily and then complain when we put on weight. We cannot attend college and never read a book or do assignments and still expect first class passes. There are seeds we need to sow so that we can get a harvest.

I look at my life and realise that this verse about the blade and the ear is an absolute God-send. God does not bring our harvest the day we sow the seed just like he did not allow the Israelites to get rid of all their enemies in one fell swoop (Judges 3)! After we sow we have to go through a time of waiting and expecting, we go through a time of knowing that something good is coming but we have to wait for it and prepare for it. This waiting time is hard. We get impatient for the goodies coming our way and sometimes we sabotage our destinies by trying to shorten the waiting time or interfering with the order God has already set in place. But we need time to grow up and mature, we need time to train our character so that we can be honourable stewards and custodians of the things God will entrust into our care. Our spirits need to be trained to be strong so that we won't be destroyed by the blessings. For this reason then God allows the seed time underground, then he lets the blade come through and finally the rest of it, the whole head then comes through and we can reap our harvest.

He is a God who has soaked our lives in his order. If we don't derail his plans by being impatient, we can benefit from them; getting a harvest that is ready for us. The nations who have not been totally destroyed become instruments of our training, sharpening our skills and character for the time we become parents, home owners, landlords, company directors and leaders in whatever spheres of influence God is bringing us to.

Picture what happens when a woman finds out that she is pregnant. Her belly does not grow immediately. Instead it grows gradually giving the skin time to stretch and accommodate the growing baby. The parents to be if they are wise make use of that nine-month gestation period to prepare a nursery, buy baby clothes, make financial arrangements, organize time off work, register with a midwife and obstetrician, adjust their diet and make sure the mother-to-be is healthy. The waiting may appear long but it is enough time for preparations to be made for the baby.

I've been reading the book of 1 Chronicles and it's amazing just how much we can learn from a book that mainly lists genealogies and job descriptions. This book gives us such insight into the mind and heart of our heavenly father. We are effective not when we are rigid and legalistic but when there is order, patterns, plans, direction. Why would God 'order' our steps (Psalm 37:23; Proverbs 16:9) and direct our paths (Proverbs 3:6) if he didn't care where we went and how? He is the God of order (1 Corinthians 14:33, Genesis 1).

In Genesis 1:2 we read the account of creation:

Now the earth was formless and empty, darkness was over the surface of the deep, and the Spirit of God was hovering over the waters

God showed up over a formless world. He started speaking over it and in so doing created order as he separated some things, made some demarcations, created sources of light and so on. Since we are as he is, we are supposed to do the same in our lives as well. When there is chaos in our lives, when things are not working out, like him we should speak into them and speak what we want to see, we can speak light when darkness seems to try and overwhelm our lives. When lack, sickness and whatever life issues assail us, we should also speak God's word over them and bring into our lives health and wealth, and whatever else we need. That is such a comforting thing, that I can speak and things happen and also that God will not honour what other people say but that I have what I say (Mark 11:24).

Here is more evidence of our God of order:

Lift up your eyes and look to the heavens: Who created all these? He who brings out the starry host one by one and calls forth each of them by name. Because of his great power and mighty strength, not one of them is missing (Isaiah 40:26)

To the human eye creation might appear random but we can't match it regardless of our levels of intelligence, education or creativity. God created a beautiful order and patterns which we take for granted; day and night, summer, winter, autumn (fall) and spring, light and dark, the tide, waves, the sky, the earth, the atmosphere. He looked at all he created and said that it was 'good' (Genesis 1:4, 10, 12, 18, 21, 25, 31). He looked it over and in his all-seeing eye it was all good. If we put our criticizing minds aside, we can see just how good God's orderly creation is. Over the centuries we have tried and are still trying to decipher the intricacy and complexity of what God made, and we are nowhere near comprehending even a significant fraction of it. God created an awesome world and gave it to us to reap its amazing rewards. He is a God of order, whether people acknowledge this or not and try to credit his handiwork to science, explosions and whatever other weird theories the human mind conceives. He bequeathed an awesome gift of an ordered world to us.

It's actually funny that I have included this chapter in this book. Maybe I am writing it to me. I am not a very tidy person, regardless of how hard I try, I can tidy up my workspace but the order usually lasts a day or two then it is back to my organised chaos. It's also weird that I am like that because I was raised by a neat freak. My mother was tidy to a fault, I know because my body received some serious correction for failing to meet her standards. Maybe my messiness started in rebellion to the exacting standards I could never meet. So I have turned out to be a direct contrast to my mother. For me to talk about order might be a bit hypocritical but then I believe in calling those things that be not as though they are (Romans 4:17), I am after all a woman of faith, faith in the God of order!

Conclusion

SOAK IT!

Life will throw curveballs at everyone. It can be complicated and it can definitely be messy. But our loving father has not left us witless or clueless. He loves us too much to leave us to our own human devices. He has promised that he will not leave us nor forsake us (Hebrews 13:5; Joshua 1:5; Deuteronomy 31:6). This tells me that regardless of what is happening in my life, he is there. Regardless of what storms I'm dealing with, he is on that boat with me (Mark 4:38). He walks with me through the valley of the shadow of death (Psalm 23) and through whatever issues I am dealing with.

What's even more exciting is the fact that we are already assured that nothing we are going through is new (Ecclesiastes 1:9) or specific only to us. Others have passed through it and we can learn from them how to get through. Even if their voices are jumbled up because of the pain, anger, regret, shame, rejection, abuse or whatever has been attacking them, God has made sure we have his word to look to. So if the witnesses are silent, God's word certainly isn't, it is alive (Hebrews 4:12). He provides relevant answers to each issue, help for each problem, strength for each challenge and solutions for all the quandaries and mazes we find ourselves in.

There is no need for us to lose hope. Yes we may struggle and we may feel tired and discouraged, but we must never lose hope. There is always a solution to every problem. We just may not see it when we are in the thick of things. This is why the soaking is so critical. We can't rush into decisions in times of fear and worry when the pressure is high. We have to soak the hard stuff is prayer, in faith, in persistence, in his presence. We have to leave our issues soaked in the Word until an answer comes through and all the gunk dissolves and all the fat floats.

Fear is really horrible when it surrounds you because it makes you feel both helpless and desperate. It is irrational because it usually cannot really be justified, more so in those of us who claim to be people of faith. It can easily derail you from the things you know you should do. It makes women compromise in their choice of a life-mate because they *fear* they may be alone for life. It makes people borrow what they can't pay back because they *fear* they can't fit in if they don't dress like everybody else. It prevents people from seeing good in others because they *fear* they may be taken for granted or their hearts may be broken yet again. Fear is like a cork that seals the bottle that is your heart, stopping access into it based on what may have happened in the past. But fear cannot be present where faith, hope and trust are. If you soak your life in faith then you won't need to be entertaining fear. It's an either/or situation. Faith or fear, the choice is yours.

God is not expecting us to come to him perfected and faultless. He knows we are human, he understands our failing. What he expects is for us to come to him, to soak our lives in his presence, his love, his goodness and his virtue. He does not want us walking around in fear because he is with us; we can soak our lives in the peace that comes from him knowing that we are surrounded by his everlasting arms (Deuteronomy 33:27). We can't believe that God is with us and still be afraid. Fear means that we are trusting in ourselves and we have looked at the issue and realised that it is too big or too strong for us. If we know that God is omnipotent then we also know that there is nothing that is too big or too hard or to frightening for him to handle.

God is not intimidated by our circumstances nor is he put off by our weakness. This is what his word says:

His strength is made perfect in weakness (2 Corinthians 12:9)

Our smallness, our limited capabilities, our humanity all contrast with God's omnipotence. We are limited where he is limitless. We are human where he is divine. We are weak where he is strong.

Let me leave you with this final thought. Life happens. It brings good and sometimes bad things tag along. The choices we all make can result in good or bad outcomes. The choices made by the people in our lives can also lead to bad outcomes for them and also for us. The environments we live in can sometimes be unkind to us. Regardless of whether you are dealing with self-made issues or those caused by others, you need to find solutions. Rush decisions hardly ever lead to meaningful solutions. Off the cuff responses hardly ever solve the stuff we are dealing with. Tough issues need tough attention. They don't need you to be flippant or to be silly in how you address them. They are tough enough to steal your peace or your sleep and they also need solutions that match the toughness of the issues. Soak the thing in a strong or concentrated enough detergent that will melt away the fat and soften the gunge. Give it enough time for it to be dealt with effectively.

Engage peace, virtue, goodness, the Word, persistence, obedience, faith or whatever you can find in God's word. Go to battle like Joshua until you wipe out the issue. Don't give up or cave in. Don't allow fear to overwhelm you and deprive you of the joy of The Lord which is where your strength comes from (Nehemiah 8:10). Soak it!

Fari's Corner

Let me share my thoughts on life and its challenges. It is very easy to focus so much on the challenges that you don't see anything else. The more you focus on them the less you see of anything positive happening around you. This is a ploy of the enemy, to keep you bound and stop you celebrating the good things that are happening in your life even while the challenges are also clamouring for your attention and time.

Here is something I have learned; you can't keep blaming other people for your pain even if they caused it. The reason why this is counterproductive is because you are the one that is living with the pain until you decide to deal with it. So regardless of how badly you have been treated, you still need to be the one that decides to find a solution so that your life can move on. Bitterness does not heal; in fact it can't heal because it is one of the contributors to your pain. Anger and hatred also don't heal; they don't have the relevant virtue in them to get you from where you are to a place of wholeness. Refusing to forgive does not destroy the person you hold a grudge against simply because the emotions reside inside you so they destroy the vessel that houses them.

Take time to address the challenges. Get some good people to help you, pray for and with you and advise you in a Godly way.

Make a decision, choose to live free of the baggage brought on by your mistakes or by the actions of others. Find scriptures that stir up your faith again to believe that God can and will help you and spend time reading the Word and feeding your spirit. Choose not to dwell in a place where you are not growing, where there is no value added to your life. Don't be in a hurry, do whatever needs to be done until you are in a good place again. You owe it to yourself to travel light. Ditch the pain, the fear, anger, unforgiveness, foolishness, bitterness, envy and anything else that is stunting your growth and slowing your progress. God loves you beyond measure and his arms are stretched out to receive you, nurture you, sustain you, strengthen you and heal you. So make the move. Do what you know you must do. SOAK IT!

Other books by Farikanayi:

Sarai-Sarah-Hall of Faith (currently being re-written)

The Shells that Shaped My Life

Hey Sal!

Hunger (Contributor)

I would love to hear from you:
farikanayi@gmail.com
https://www.facebook.com/Farikanayi